Twayne's English Authors Series

Sylvia E. Bowman, *Editor*

INDIANA UNIVERSITY

John Lyly

TEAS 177

John Lyly

By JOSEPH W. HOUPPERT
University of Maryland

TWAYNE PUBLISHERS
A DIVISION OF G. K. HALL & CO., BOSTON

Library of Congress Cataloging in Publication Data

Houppert, Joseph W
  John Lyly.

  (Twayne's English authors series; TEAS 177)
  Bibliography: p. 159-62.
  Includes index.
  1. Lyly, John, 1554?-1606.
PR2303.H6   828'.3'09   74-20932
ISBN 0-8057-1349-2

PR
2303
.H6

66758

For Maureen
Elizabeth
Anne
David

Contents

About the Author

Joseph W. Houppert received his Ph.B. from the University of Detroit (1956), his M.A. and Ph.D. from the University of Michigan (1957, 1964). He taught three years at the University of Michigan as a Teaching Fellow, and came to the University of Maryland in 1962 as an Instructor; he is currently an Associate Professor.

In 1965 Mr. Houppert published "Thomas Lodge's Letters to William Trumbull," *Renaissance News*, XVIII (1965), 118-23. This was followed in 1968 by *Cardinal Newman*, B. Herder Co., a collection of essays which he edited as part of the Christian Critics Series. *Thomas Lodge's The Wounds of Civil War*, prepared for the Regents Renaissance Drama Series (University of Nebraska Press) was published in 1969. In 1973, the author contributed "John Lyly" and "Thomas Lodge," two bibliographical essays, to *The Predecessors of Shakespeare*, ed. Terence P. Logan and Denzell S. Smith (University of Nebraska Press, pp. 125-43, 153-60). "Fatal Logic in *Julius Caesar*," *South Atlantic Bulletin*, xxxix (1974), 3-9 appeared in 1974.

Preface

This book about John Lyly is addressed to students and teachers who, although not specialists in sixteenth-century literature, are interested in Elizabethan literature. My purpose is twofold: (1) to analyze the prose narratives in terms of Lyly's unique ironic vision, which is so effectively communicated through his Euphuistic style, and (2) to analyze the plays in terms of the dramatic tradition from which they arose but to stress Lyly's independence in the face of that tradition. The notes have been keyed to popular editions of Lyly's works rather than to the original sixteenth-century editions because these are inaccessible, except in specialized libraries.

Since such matters as biography, the development of Euphuism, and the history of personages supposedly alluded to in the plays have been treated at length elsewhere (see Bibliography), little is said about these aspects. I have not discussed Lyly's political writings, nor have I investigated the problem of entertainments possibly written by Lyly, not because these matters are unimportant, but because the exigencies of space prohibit such luxuries.

The first chapter provides a brief biography and an overview of Lyly's belletristic writings. The second chapter analyzes the prose narratives, *Euphues, the Anatomy of Wit* and *Euphues and His England.* Chapters 3 through 5 examine the plays in their presumed order of composition; but since the dating of the plays is tentative, the ordering is, at best, conjectural. Chapter 6 presents the plays and the critics, and Chapter 7 assesses Lyly's reputation and influence.

I would like to thank the librarians at the Folger Shakespeare Library for their assistance and the University of Maryland Research Board for financial aid. Finally, I would like to express my gratitude to Professor Sylvia Bowman for her patience and expert editorial assistance, and to my wife, Maureen, for her continual support and encouragement.

JOSEPH W. HOUPPERT

University of Maryland

Chronology

1553?   John Lyly, grandson of the grammarian William Lily, born probably in Kent.

1569   Enters Magdalen College, Oxford.

1573   Bachelor of Arts, Oxford.

1575   Master of Arts, Oxford.

1578   *Euphues: The Anatomy of Wit.*

1579   Master of Arts (by incorporation), Cambridge.

1580   *Euphues and His England.*

1583   Marries Beatrice Brown. Receives lease to Blackfriars Theater from the Earl of Oxford, in whose service Lyly was inscribed throughout most of the 1580's.

1583-
1584?   *Campaspe, Sapho and Phao.*

1587-
1588?   *Gallathea, Endimion.*

1588-
1590?   *Loves Metamorphosis*

1589   *Pappe with an Hatchet.* Member of Parliament for Hindon.

1589-
1590?   *Midas*

1591-
1595?   *The Woman in the Moon.*

1590's?   *Mother Bombie.*

1593   Member of Parliament for Aylesbury.

1597   Member of Parliament for Appleby.

1601   Member of Parliament for Aylesbury.

1606   Death of John Lyly

CHAPTER 1

John Lyly: An Overview

JOHN Lyly, son of Peter Lyly and grandson of the famous Humanist grammarian William Lily, was probably born and was certainly reared in Canterbury, "an old city somewhat decayed yet beautiful to behold; most famous for a Cathedral Church."[1] He very likely attended the Cathedral Grammar School where he would have been exposed to the Latin writers who later influenced his writing—Plutarch, Ovid, and Pliny. There he would also have been introduced to the ancient study of rhetoric, and of the schemes and tropes that were to form the basis, along with his complex vision of reality, of his Euphuistic style.

According to Anthony à Wood, Lyly matriculated at Magdalen College, Oxford, in 1569; but the College Register records the year as 1571. Since Lyly supplicated for the Bachelor of Arts degree in 1573, an event which ordinarily occurred four years after matriculation, à Wood seems to be correct. At Magdalen College, Lyly may have listened to Dr. John Rainolds, a lecturer whose Latin orations may have been the most formative influence on Lyly's Euphuistic style.[2] Seemingly, Lyly also came under the influence of less august persons than Rainold; for Gabriel Harvey, a Cambridge Humanist, later referred to Lyly as "the fiddlestick of Oxford."[3] In 1574 a series of disappointments began when Lyly asked Lord Burghley, to whom he was distantly related, to support his application to be admitted to Magdalen College as a Fellow. Lyly was rejected, just as he was rejected for almost every significant position, including that of Master of the Revels, for which he sued throughout his career.

In 1575, Lyly was awarded the Master of Arts degree; and he followed the lead of other would-be writers by traveling to London. There, on December 2, 1578, a book entitled *Euphues, the Anatomy of Wit*, was entered in the *Stationers Register;* and the work published shortly thereafter. Two years later appeared a sequel entitled *Euphues and His England*. After Lyly's arrival in London, he became secretary to the notorious Edward de Vere, the seventeenth Earl of Oxford, a position which undoubtedly enhanced his literary potential. De Vere was himself a poet and playwright, although no plays bearing his name survive. More important for Lyly, however, was the fact that the position made available to him both the company of boy actors under de Vere's patronage (Lord Oxford's Boys) and the Blackfriars Theatre.

For about ten years, from 1580 to 1590, with time off for marriage to Beatrice Brown in 1583, Lyly wrote comedies for the private stage. But in the early 1590's he ceased writing plays and entertainments; and, during the last twelve or fifteen years of his life, he produced no belletristic works (Lyly may have composed *The Entertainment at Mitcham* as late as 1598, but the case for his authorship is uncertain).[4] He did, however, flourish as a minor political figure, as a Member of Parliament from a variety of boroughs. His departure from the stage may have been occasioned by public disapproval since the Euphuistic style, which had served him so well in the 1580's, had become an object of ridicule by 1600, as is clearly evident from the use to which Shakespeare puts it in *I Henry IV*.[5] But Lyly's rejection came only after considerable fame, as evidenced by the high praise accorded him by Francis Meres, who includes him in a list of playwrights who are "the best for comedy amongst us."[6] Compared to William Shakespeare or Edmund Spenser, Lyly's literary output was slight. The royal promotions and pensions he so ardently sought were continually denied him. His fame as a literary stylist was short indeed. Yet he married well, and lived his life in comfortable, if not lavish, circumstances.

I   *The Works*

By the last two decades of the sixteenth century, English prose had established itself as an enduring vehicle in spite of the concern shown by such astute observers as Sir Francis Bacon, who, even after 1600, would write, "These modern languages will play the bank-route with books."[7] However, most Elizabethans agreed with Richard Mulcaster's verdict: "I do not think that any language, be it whatsoever, is beter able to utter all arguments, either with more pith, or greater planesse than our English tung is, if the English utterer be as skilfull in the matter, which he is to utter: as the foren utterer is."[8]

But the English "tung" of the late sixteenth century was remarkably different from that of the late fifteenth or even early sixteenth century. Readers who have little difficulty following Lyly's Euphuistic style are often distressed by the style of Thomas More or John Colet. Lyly is amazingly modern, right down to his vocabulary—the dictionary is seldom required. Allusions are frequently obscure, as is the unnatural natural history; but the words themselves pose little difficulty, probably less so than in any other Elizabethan writer.

Although Lyly's vocabulary and syntax pose no great obstacles to modern readers, his narrative technique does so. The most prevalent criticism is that Lyly moralizes interminably and that he keeps interrupting the narratives with authorial comments. But, in this respect, Lyly was simply a man of his times. Most of what passed for fiction in the last third of the sixteenth century suffers from the same kind of moralization. George Gascoigne's *Adventures of Master F. J.* (1573), George Whetstone's *The Rock of Regard* (1576), John Grange's *Golden Aphrodite* (1577), Stephen Gosson's *Ephermerides of Phialo* (1579), Austin Saker's *Narbonus* (1580)—all popular narratives of the period—are filled with interminable moralizing. Interminable, that is, to a modern temperament but not to a sixteenth-century mind which liked its fiction heavily spiced with morality. Two of the most highly regarded literary works of the Elizabethan Age, Edmund Spenser's *Faerie Queene* and Sir Philip Sidney's *Arcadia*, are both given to ready moralizing. In fact, Sidney's great contribution to the pastoral romance was in the moralization of plot.[9] Thus, to inveigh against Lyly's moralizing is to castigate the central thrust of Elizabethan fiction.

To compound the difficulty posed by the moralizing, Lyly wrote for an audience schooled in the Classical tradition of rhetoric, a discipline no longer pursued with either vigor or enthusiasm. Only a reader trained in the same rhetorical tradition as Lyly can hope to understand fully his sometimes serious, sometimes playful, handling of the English "tung." Lyly's Euphuistic style more closely resembles a Bach fugue than a Beethoven symphony, and readers reared on Romantic theories of self-expression are likely to miss the subtleties. When the felicities pass unnoticed, the moralizing is apt to cloy.

Indeed, Lyly's appeal to the readers of his own era is clear. *Euphues, the Anatomy of Wit* passed through thirteen editions by 1613, and *Euphues and His England* through twelve by 1609—an admirable publishing record when one considers that Thomas Lodge's *Rosalynde*, the most popular pastoral romance of the period, passed through only seven editions during Lodge's lifetime. Yet Lyly's audience was narrow, at least by modern standards. The sermons of the Reverend Henry Smith, rector of St. Clement's Dane in London, passed through a hundred and twenty-seven editions in various forms between 1589 and 1640, thereby attesting to the reading tastes of most Londoners.[10]

II *Euphuism*

When *Euphues* burst upon the London literary scene in 1578, Lyly's fame was assured. That "fatal success," as C. S. Lewis referred to it,[11] created a vogue which lasted for about fifteen years; and it resulted not only in Lyly's own sequel, *Euphues and His England*, but also in a whole spate of Euphuistic romances, including such notable efforts as Robert Greene's *Pandosto* and Thomas Lodge's *Rosalynde*. The style which Lyly created made him famous, but the fame was short-lived, for by the end of the century, Euphuism as a viable literary style had been all but eclipsed by less "elegant" forms of expression.

Euphuism consists of balance, antithesis, parallelism, alliteration, assonance, and rhyme; in short, in corresponding members of both sound and sense. It consists also of elaborate images and involved allusions from mythology and unnatural natural history. Yet none of these was new to English prose style; these rhetorical devices can be found in Thomas More, in George Pettie, and in a whole line of preceptors who stretch back to the Greek rhetoricians. Even the allusions from unnatural natural history were not unique, for copious examples appear in Thomas Malory and Geoffrey Chaucer.

In spite of Lyly's reliance upon the work of others, he nevertheless created a unique style. One has only to compare Lyly with his predecessors or his imitators to detect the uniqueness. His is one of the few cases in literary history in which quantity determines quality, for the essence of his uniqueness lies, in part at least, in his unrelenting use of rhetorical figures that are used more sparingly by other writers. Thomas More before him and Thomas Browne after him used sentences based on antitheses and parallelisms, but they used them sparingly. Almost every single sentence that Lyly writes in the narratives is based on antithesis and parallelism.

Yet, when all of this has been said, something is still missing. To understand Lyly's uniqueness is also to understand his complex view of reality: "But as the chameleon though he have most guts draweth least breath or as the elder tree though he be fullest of pith is farthest from strength, so though your reasons seem inwardly to yourself somewhat substantial and your persuasions pithy in your own conceit, yet being well weighed without they be shadows without substance and weak without force" (*Euphues*, 24). This characteristic sentence contains all of the elements usually associated with Lyly—balance, antithesis, alliteration, assonance, etc. But this passage also contains, or expresses, a view of reality which is rooted in complexity. What is remarkable about Lyly's unnatural history is not that the examples are usually fabulous but that they testify to a paradoxical universe. Since the chameleon has the largest intestine, one would expect him to breathe the deepest—yet he breathes the least. Since the elder tree is the broadest, one would expect it to be the strongest—yet it is the weakest. Lyly is saying that it is easy to be deceived by appearances.

Lyly's principal theme throughout his works, in fact, is the distinction between appearance and reality. Deception is not the prerogative of lizards and trees—men are also very good at it. The difference is that men practice it by design; natural creatures, by instinct. Nature cannot help herself, but man can, by exercise of his will, control his wayward tendencies. And by exercise of will Lyly means education evolving from experience, for it above all else ultimately outfits a man for his role in life. Experience, and experience alone, teaches man to discern the real from the apparent good. Wit versus wisdom—the former, the curse of youth; the latter, the blessing of age—is an important theme in both *Euphues* and *Euphues and His England*.

Until quite recently most Lyly critics focused on the sources of Euphuism. Among the more influential studies in this area must be included F. Landmann's *Euphuismus* (1881) in German; J. Dover

Wilson's *John Lyly* (1905) in English; and Albert Feuillerat's *John Lyly* (1910) in French. Perhaps the most influential study for English-speaking readers of Lyly is Morris W. Croll's Introduction to the edition of *Euphues* and *Euphues and His England* which he co-edited with Harry Clemons (1916).[12]

The most perceptive of the recent studies is that of Jonas Barish, who argues against Morris Croll's dichotomy of sound and sense and who claims that "parison, far from being merely a superficial device of sound-design, is, one might almost say, an instrument of thought whereby Lyly apprehends the world, and from which he cannot escape."[13] Barish believes that Lyly's style aims at expressing a world full of paradoxes and contradictions and that the antithetical style is itself a reflection of this world. Lyly likes to play with predictable correspondences, such as the appearance-reality complex, and to overthrow them in order to establish a new assumption. And the result of these new assumptions is an overall assumption about the nature of the universe, one that it is, in fact, a universal paradox. "This commanding insight," Barish argues, "is perhaps the chief thing that distinguishes Lyly from his predecessors in Euphuism."[14] The picture of Lyly's world that emerges is that of an intellectual universe far richer and more complex than critics have hitherto imagined.

Lyly's style actually functions on two or three levels. From the point of view of rhetoric, it reveals a thorough grounding in the tropes, in the schemes of Medieval and Renaissance theory, and in the syntax of Latin grammar. At the same time, however, it reveals a playfulness with language that is missing in Lyly's predecessors. No writer before Lyly—and none with the exception of James Joyce after him—took such delight in the combinations and permutations which can be effected by the sound and sense of the English language. No other writer takes such obvious delight in playing with sentences such as the following one from *Euphues:* "Thou weepest for the death of thy daughter, and I laugh at the folly of the father; for greater vanity is there in the mind of the mourner, than bitterness in the death of the deceased" (168). All the devices usually associated with Lyly are present in this sentence: balance, parallelism, antithesis, assonance, alliteration, rhyme. The first sentence element—*Thou weepest for the death of thy daughter*—is eight words in length, as is the second element—*I laugh at the folly of the father.* The first element is ten syllables in length, as is the second. The first element presents subject followed by predicate—*Thou weepest*—followed by two prepositional phrases, (1) *for the death*, (2) *of thy daughter.* The second element presents subject followed by predicate—*I laugh*—and is followed by two prepositional phrases; (1) *at the folly*, (2) *of the father.* Each subject-predicate unit is composed of two words, and each of the four clauses is composed of four. In the first element, the last word of the first phrase alliterates with the last word of the second—*death . . . daughter;* and the pattern is similarly observed in the second element—*folly . . . father.* The same relationships are observed in the rest of the quotation, but more important than these correspondences is the view of reality which emerges from the I—thou antithesis.

The three key words in the first element—*weepest, death, daughter*—present nothing unusual; in fact, one expects them. In the second element, however, Lyly rings the changes as the first two key words—*laugh, folly*—do not relate in the same way to the third, *father.* For the father to weep at the death of the daughter is expected, but for the observer to laugh at the folly of the father who weeps for the daughter appears cruel and sadistic. Appears, that is, until one sees what Lyly is about! For in the third element—*for greater vanity is there in the mind of the mourner*—the first key word—*vanity*—clashes with the second and third—*mind, mourner;* but in the fourth element—*than bitterness in the death of the deceased*—one returns to the arrangement of terms which one found in the first element, as the three key words harmoniously relate—*bitterness, death, deceased.* One expects bitterness on the occasion of death, just as one expects tears. One does not, however, expect to find mourners described as vain any more than one expects to find weeping fathers described as foolish. Yet it is out of this kind of paradox that Lyly's peculiar vision emerges.

For, as one sees in the context of the novel, Eubulus, to whom these words are addressed, is being foolish and vain because he has forgotten his place in the scheme of things. The Christian story, in whose vortex Eubulus's fate is worked out, is itself a paradox; for Christianity proclaims that, unless a man dies, he may not live. Against this background, Lyly's lines must be interpreted; and, when one views them in this way, one sees the profound reality behind the appearance of mere cleverness. The true Christian must look upon death as a joyful, not as a sad, event; but his own estimate of himself leads readily to an exalted notion of his own importance. His vanity, in other words, encourages him to assume a foolish pose in the face of the only reality worth considering.

There is, then, a structure in this sentence unit which reflects the structure of the work at large. Paradox works itself out within harmony—the discordant second and third sentence elements are bound in by the harmonious first and fourth—just as evil works itself out within the divine plan of God. Euphues's advice to Eubulus not to weep for the death of his daughter is thus communicated by a combination of language and structure. The advice of the true Christian is more than merely a trite remedy for grief. Through his unique fusion of sound and sense, Lyly is able to say what has been said a thousand times before; but he says it in an original and forceful way.

This structural principle is lost by Lyly's imitators, for they usually recapture some of the superficial ingredients, the balance, antithesis, etc. They occasionally catch at the spirit of paradox which antithesis encourages; they never, however, recapture Lyly's vision of a world in which paradox is bound in by harmony—a vision that is closer in spirit to Spenser's *Mutability Cantos* than to anything Greene or Lodge ever wrote.

Just how much of Lyly's Euphuism carries over to his plays is difficult to calculate. The vision is present, but the vehicle is different. Some critics, such as R. W. Bond, argue that Lyly abandoned Euphuism when he turned to the stage. Other critics, such as Geoffrey Tillotson, suggest that Lyly's "developed sense of the English language was a sense of the rhythms of words in combination, and of the associations and colours of words when combined in small or large groups, i.e. in phrases or in a play as a whole."[15] Zdenek Stríbrný claims that Lyly's Euphuistic style is manifested in the plays in the form of balanced structure, antithetical groups of characters; in short, Lyly transferred the main principles of Euphuism from the sphere of style into a higher sphere of composition.[16] Jonas Barish believes that the comedies share the same style as the narratives except that many of the devices of sound-design have been dropped. Barish sees Lyly as a revolutionary who "invented, virtually single-handed, a viable comic prose for the

English stage, something which could replace the clumsy, uncertain medium of Gascoigne's *Supposes*."[17]

Peter Saccio, who takes Barish's thesis a giant step forward, describes the Euphuism in *Campaspe* as neither the isocolon-parison figure of Croll nor the grammatical patterns of antithesis and parallelism of Barish. Instead, Saccio says, the basic unit of expression is a statement of identity or attribution: "The play abounds in remarks of the form, '*a* is *b*,' where *b* is a noun or adjective in the nominative case and the statement is intended to isolate a central aspect of *a*; and of the form, '*a* does *b*,' where doing *b* is conceived of as an action particularly characteristic of *a*."[18]

Saccio's analysis leads finally to the following definition of Lyly's dramatic Euphuism: "It is founded on definitions, the definitions are placed in juxtaposition, and the dialogue moves through the pattern of juxtaposition setting it in order. It is a vigorous style; it is a factual and intellectual style."[19] Saccio concludes that Lyly's style "is a tool superbly fitted for the intellectual exploration of a complex world."[20] But, in trying to demonstrate the complexity of Lyly's world view, Saccio assumes the truth of what he is trying to prove. To say that Lyly explores a complex world is inaccurate, for Lyly's world is complex *because* of the way he describes it; that is, Lyly's Euphuistic style communicates a complex experience or apprehension of the world.

However Lyly's style is approached, it remains one of the outstanding phenomena of Western literature. And, whatever his faults, the fact remains that he performed a great service on behalf of English prose. He gave to fiction a delicacy hitherto unknown and to drama a sophistication through which it could delineate character and explore theme with facility and detachment.

CHAPTER 2

Non-Dramatic Fiction

I Euphues, the Anatomy of Wit

E UPHUES, the Anatomy of Wit, an adventure story, is about a "student's progress" in maturation in an alien, vicious culture. Although Euphues temporarily falls victim to disenchantment and naivete, he overcomes in true-blue English fashion, after a long struggle and great personal sacrifice, the malevolent influences around him and retires to a life of solitude and study. Yet the ironic thrust of the narrative is clear: courtly morality blinds Euphues to the immorality of the court where self-indulgence masquerades as love, betrayal as cleverness, and meanness of spirit as sophistication.

Unfortunately, Lyly's inventive powers were not such that he could sustain a continuous narrative; the plot of *Euphues,* instead of serving as a vehicle to illustrate character or to develop a theme, serves as a thread on which Lyly hangs a number of fashionable topics—youth opposed to age; wit, to wisdom; friendship, to love. Actually, as will be demonstrated later, Lyly's powers as an embryo novelist continued to develop so that *Euphues and His England* is a far more satisfying artistic achievement; and, ironically, Lyly is best known for his least perfect narrative. As a sequel, *Euphues and His England* may be unique in that it surpasses its prototype.

Many critics have denied that *Euphues* is structurally sound.[1] G. K. Hunter, arguing against these critics, attempts to demonstrate that the structure of *Euphues* approximates the five-act form of Terentian comedy:

The first 'act' concerns Euphues's arrival in Naples. . . . In Act II we meet Philautus, and hear the pledges of friendship that the two men make, . . . The stage is cleared; we leave the house of Lucilla . . . 'and return we to

Euphues. . . .' The act [i.e., Act III] ends with the departure of Euphues. . . . In Act IV Ferardo and Philautus return to Naples; Ferardo proposes that Philautus should marry Lucilla straight away; Lucilla prevaricates and finally names Euphues as already in possession of her heart; Philautus returns to his lodging, inveighs against Euphues and writes a letter of reproach; as a pendant to this comes Euphues's letter of reply. . . . In Act V Euphues visits Lucilla, and is told that his love is no longer acceptable; left alone he renounces wit, except when 'employed in the honest study of learning'; Ferardo returns home 'immediately' and rates his daughter with her inconstancy; in a final narrative passage we hear of the eventual reconcilement of Euphues and Philautus.

The 'five-act structure' I have been describing here would hardly be worth pursuing in such detail if it only involved moving the characters around, . . . But I think we can see in *Euphues* the rise and fall of the Terentian structure, used in a manner which shapes the whole experience. Through the acts we can see the underlying pattern of Protasis, Epitasis and Catastrophe—or (in more modern terms) exposition, action, complication, reversal, catastrophe. Lyly's plays show that he was well aware of this structure, . . .[2]

Although ingenious, Hunter's argument fails at crucial points. The first act of a Terentian comedy provides exposition; the "first act" of *Euphues* does not. True, the characters of Euphues and Eubulus are introduced, but almost nothing by way of essential information is exposed. The story of *Euphues* begins at the beginning; no exposition is required. Furthermore, Hunter's contention that a new act begins when the stage is cleared breaks down in *Euphues*. Every time Lyly brings characters together in dramatic confrontations, he follows with an interlude which clears the stage. Such clearing occurs, in fact, seven times in the narrative, yet no one has claimed that *Euphues* is a seven-act narrative.

Finally, one might ask G. K. Hunter what advantage is to be gained from approaching *Euphues*—or any narrative—from the point of view of the stage? The demands of drama and narrative fiction are radically different; the styles are entirely dissimilar. Drama is to be seen and heard; narrative fiction to be read. The convoluted Euphuistic sentences so abundant in *Euphues* are seldom found in the plays. In *Euphues*, Lyly combines a number of styles—straight narrative, didactic, epistolary—and forms—monologue, dialogue—

into a narrative structure that not only permits but also encourages such intermingling. In stage plays, on the contrary, dialogue is the staple.

It appears likely that Lyly was experimenting in *Euphues* with a framework constructed of dramatic encounters separated by interludes of various kinds. The first encounter, between Euphues and Eubulus, is followed by moral reflections by the author; the second, between Euphues and Philautus, by the reflections of Euphues and Lucilla; and the third, again between Euphues and Philautus, by further moral reflections of the author. The fourth and fifth encounters are the most dramatic, since they include more participants and less debate. The fourth, between Euphues, Philautus, Lucilla, and Livia, is followed by a brief summation of the action by the author; and the fifth, between Ferardo, Lucilla, and Philautus, is followed by an exchange of letters between Euphues and Philautus. The sixth encounter, between Euphues and Lucilla, is followed by Euphues's lament over the loss of Lucilla; and the seventh encounter, between Lucilla and Ferardo, is followed by the reconciliation, described in narrative form by the author, of Euphues and Philautus. It may be pure coincidence that the narrative ends with a series of *seven* letters—and then again it may not.

Lyly develops his multitudinous themes or topics in *Euphues* through a series of encounters generally involving Euphues and one or two other characters. From the first encounter, with Eubulus, to the final reconciliation between Euphues and Philautus, the protagonist grows in understanding and wisdom. The young man who at the beginning is described as "of more wit than wrath, and yet of more wrath than wisdom" (10) is by the end able to reject the world and all it represents. The young man who at the beginning replies to the sage advice of Eubulus with scorn is by the end able to advise Atheos to "fly unto that Christ which hath through His mercy, not our merits, purchased for us the inheritance of everlasting life" (162).

Euphues's journey introduces the reader to a highly urbane, sophisticated culture, one populated by courtiers and their ladies with an occasional hermit added for the sake of edification. One finds in *Euphues* none of the grim realism which characterizes the later prose fiction of Greene and Deloney, unless it be grim psychological realism—of this there is plenty. Yet both Greene and Lyly share a sociological bent, for both attempt to record the vagaries of English social classes; Greene, the Elizabethan underworld; Lyly, courtly high life. Yet in both social classes a hierarchy of values obtains, so that Greene's conies are often reflected in Euphues and in Philautus who also pursue false goals.

In Lyly's attempt to lay bare the manners and morals of a courtly society, he suspects that he might eventually tread on hallowed ground; he feels that a defense is required. He therefore calls upon the traditional Humanist argument that just as the rose must be represented with its thorns, so must man be represented, if truth is to be a standard of judgment, with his moral deformities. Then, employing the artistic notion that the end justifies the means, Lyly uses the moralist's argument to anticipate objections against his subject matter:

If then the first sight of Euphues shall seem too light to be read of the wise or too foolish to be regarded of the learned, they ought not to impute it to the iniquity of the author but to the necessity of the history. Euphues beginneth with love as allured by wit, but endeth not with lust as bereft of wisdom. He wooeth women provoked by youth, but weddeth not himself to wantonness as pricked by pleasure. I have set down the follies of his wit without breach of modesty and the sparks of his wisdom without suspicion of dishonesty. And, certes, I think there be more speeches which for gravity will mislike the foolish than unseemly terms which for vanity may offend the wise. (5)

To an age nurtured on Henry Miller, nothing in *Euphues* or *Euphues and His England* is shocking or morally disgusting. Yet no criticism was more strongly felt in the last quarter of the sixteenth century than Puritan criticism, such as that of Stephen Gosson. Although most of the Puritan attacks were so effectively aimed at stage plays that the theaters were expelled from the municipality of London in 1575, all poetry (which, in the sixteenth century, included prose) felt its sting. Lyly's defense is based on the Plutarchian analogy that just as the bee distills sweet honey from noxious herbs, so the poet brings sweet truth and sound morality from human failings. Gosson, however, takes a different view:

Therefore, as I cannot but commend his wisdom which in banquetting feedes most uppon that that doth nourishe best, so must I dispraise his methode in writing which, following the course of amarous poets, dwelleth longest on those points that profit least, and like a wanton whelpe leaveth the game to runne riot. The scarabe flies over many a sweet flower, and lightes in a cowsherd. It is the custome of the flie to leave the sound places of the horse, and sucke at the botch: the nature of colloquintida to draw the worst humors to it selfe: the manner of swine to forsake the fayre fields and wallowe in the myre; and the whole practise of poets, either with fables to shewe their abuses, or with playne tearmes to unfolde their mischeffe, discover their shame, discredite themselves, and disperse their poison through the world.[3]

If one multiplies Gosson's attack a hundredfold, one may easily comprehend why Lyly was so anxious to forestall objections.

Lyly provides his hero with a history, albeit a brief one. Within a page or two, the reader learns that Euphues, a young Athenian gentleman (a student at Oxford) has forsaken his homeland for Naples (London, or any other large metropolitan center of sophistication), "a place of more pleasure than profit and yet of more profit than piety," the "Tabernacle of Venus [rather] than the Temple of Vesta" (11-12). One soon discovers, however, that Euphues is no fool and that Athens is no moral paradise. Euphues survives in Athens because he cultivates, as Machiavelli recommended fifty-nine years earlier, the attributes of the animals:[4] "He behaved himself so *warily* . . . he was merry, but yet so *wary* that neither the flatterer could take advantage to entrap him in his talk nor the wisest any assurance of his friendship" (12-13; italics mine).

The hunting metaphor and the isolation theme set the tone for the opening encounter between Euphues and Eubulus, and they prepare for the theme of ruptured friendship which occupies much of the narrative. (Euphues's ability to dissimulate, also stressed in this opening section, finds its counterpart later in the story in Lucilla's superior abilities.) Euphues and Eubulus reenact the biblical tale of the wise father and the prodigal son. In fact, as J. D. Wilson points out, the greater part of *Euphues* is structured around the prodigal-son motif.[5] The encounter with Eubulus characterizes Euphues as a man with great potentiality for good or for evil. In order to insure the former, Eubulus tries to impress upon Euphues the importance of discipline in the educative process and Euphues's apparent lack of it. Nowhere in the narrative do proverbs flow with quite the same intensity as they do in Eubulus's homily: young men are like new wax, receptive to any impressed form; they are like potter's clay which is fashioned when it is soft; they are like sparrows who are taught to obey when young; they are like iron which is forged when it is hot and thereafter keeps the form which it receives. Eubulus's homily is rounded off with a series of maxims which remind one of those of Polonius in *Hamlet:*

Be merry but with modesty, be sober but not too sullen, be valiant but not too venturous. Let thy attire be comely but not costly, thy diet wholesome but not excessive, use pastime as the word importeth—to pass the time in honest recreation. Mistrust no man without cause, neither be thou credulous without proof, be not light to follow every man's opinion, nor obstinate to stand in thine own conceit. Serve God, love God, fear God, and God will so bless thee as either thy heart can wish or thy friends desire. And so I end my counsel, beseeching thee to begin to follow it. (17)

Euphues does not, however, receive Eubulus's advice with the same spirit of equanimity as Laertes received that of Polonius. In fact, Euphues attacks Eubulus; and he attacks where Eubulus is strongest. Eubulus's advice came from accumulated experiences, and Euphues regards that kind of experience as debilitating and as irrelevant to the concerns of youth. This encounter, therefore, lays the foundation for the thematic reversal which occurs later in the narrative when Euphues lectures Alcius in the same manner that he himself has been lectured here.

The first encounter ends with the wit of Euphues pitted against the wisdom of Eubulus, whose parting words prepare the reader for events to come: "Seeing thou wilt not buy counsel at the first hand good cheap, thou shalt buy repentance at the second hand at such an unreasonable rate that thou wilt curse thy hard pennyworth and ban thy hard heart" (25). It is no accident that Lyly places near the very end of *Euphues* the letter to Alcius, "who, leaving his study, followed all lightness and lived both shamefully and sinfully, to the grief of his friends and discredit of the university" (175). By the end of *Euphues*, a reversal has been effected; now Euphues, the former prodigal, reenacts the role of Eubulus, whom he so harshly criticized at the start.

The first encounter is followed by a brief interlude as the author

offers his reflections about what has just occurred. Siding with Eubulus, the author also emphasizes the necessity of discipline in
education, stressing the naïveté of "novices that think to have learning without labour and treasure without travail" (27). The reality
which lies behind Eubulus's advice regarding final things is sacrificed to the glittering, yet deceptive, world of sophistication, where
discussions of sin and damnation give way to questions of love.
Euphues now falls prey to one temptation after another as he
attempts to sift his way through a world beset with tinseled traps.

Friendship as opposed to love now becomes the principle theme
as Euphues meets Philautus, who in turn introduces him to his
fiancée, Lucilla, "more fair than fortunate, and yet more fortunate
than faithful" (32). Initially, Euphues is repelled by Lucilla; but her
beauty soon works its effect upon him, and he becomes "so kindled
with desire that almost he was like to burn to coals" (34). After a
dinner party Lucilla and her gentle ladies call for a discourse on
love or learning. To the relief and delight of a decade of readers,
Lyly followed the lead of Castiglione by having his characters discourse on love. Euphues selects as his first topic the question
"whether the qualities of the mind or the composition of the man
cause women most to like, or whether beauty or wit move men most
to love" (35). Euphues argues, possibly to disguise his own inflamed
passions, that the mind is to be preferred to the body, that the outward shape is not always indicative of the inward habit. Furthermore, physical beauty is not to be prized for "it fadeth before one
perceive it flourish," and is dangerous to the possessor because it
poisons her (36). Continuing in this anticourtly vein, Euphues
proceeds to mock the picture of the traditional courtly lover who,
although disdained by his beloved, pledges his secrecy (so that his
beloved may conceal her enticing slights) and his service (so that
she, his sovereign, may selfishly receive his entire attention).

Then, switching his attack, Euphues condemns the traditional,
coy ladies who "loved none in their youth" (37). With an eye, perhaps, on Lucilla, Euphues encourages young beauties to give freely
of themselves when they are able; and he advises them, in sound
carpe diem fashion:

When the black crow's foot shall appear in their eye or the black ox tread
on their foot, when their beauty shall be like the blasted rose, their wealth

wasted, their bodies worn, their faces wrinkled, their fingers crooked, who will like of them in their age who loved none in their youth? If you will be cherished when you be old, be courteous while you be young; if you look for comfort in your hoary hairs, be not coy when you have your golden locks; if you would be embraced in the waning of your bravery, be not squeamish in the waxing of your beauty; if you desire to be kept like the roses when they have lost their colour, smell sweet as the rose doth in the bud; if you would be tasted for old wine, be in the mouth a pleasant grape—so shall you be cherished for your courtesy, comforted for your honesty, embraced for your amity, so shall you be preserved with the sweet rose, and drunk with the pleasant wine. (37)

Having disposed of the first question of love by answering it both ways, Euphues selects as his second topic "whether man or woman be soonest allured, whether be most constant the male or the female" (37). Perhaps with the intent of trapping Lucilla, Euphues asks for her reply. Her answer, although prefiguring her subsequent unfaithfulness, is perfunctory and rooted in the misogynist tradition of the Middle Ages: "Gentlemen, in mine opinion women are to be won with every wind, in whose sex there is neither force to withstand the assaults of love, neither constancy to remain faithful" (38). She immediately returns the conversation to Euphues who, reversing himself again, argues that women crave not wantonness but reason, are not cruel but civil, not filthy but faithful. But his discourse is interrupted by an "alteration" which makes further speech impossible. Although not explicitly revealed, the "alteration" is presumably caused by the passion which has conquered Euphues. The ladies apparently interpret it in this way, for they "all changed colour" (39), or blushed, at the sudden change in Euphues.

The perplexity which has settled on Euphues is shared by Lucilla, who now begins "to fry in the flames of love" (39). Better able to dissimulate than Euphues, Lucilla is, nevertheless, unable to overcome the mutual passion which consumes them. What follows now takes the form of Lucilla's and Euphues's laments and constitutes the second encounter. The same point stressed by Euphues in his debate with Eubulus is here reiterated. Earlier, Euphues argued that a man's nature, which is essentially unalterable, determines his worth; now Lucilla uses the same argument. Since Euphues excels Philautus in good properties, she ought by *nature* to prefer him (41). At this point, however, she recalls her own reply to the second

question of love. By her own admission, women are weak and
fickle—thus she has condemned herself. Next, she considers the
social consequences of dismissing Philautus—perhaps her father
will force on her an objectionable suitor. But love—or lust—wins
out, and she surrenders to the overwhelming passion with the
proviso that she will dissemble and persuade both Euphues and
Philautus that she is faithful.

In his lament, Euphues goes beyond Lucilla in an attempt to
justify his betrayal of Philautus. Courtly love replaces nature as
Euphues argues with himself that any form of inhibition or sup-
pression increases love; therefore, reason must be exercised in order
to find a means of satisfying the cravings of love. Friendship must
not only be sacrificed to love but also be used in its service. Lucilla
will dissemble with Philautus; Euphues will use him until he finally
possesses his "saint" (45). That he will possess Lucilla there is no
doubt; for, as Euphues says, "There is no woman . . . but she will
yield in time; be not therefore dismayed either with high looks or
froward words" (48). With this misogynist evaluation ringing in
one's ears, Euphues concludes his examination of conscience; and
Lyly permits the reader to evaluate the quality of Euphues's love.

With Euphues's callous words as a background, the third encounter strikes with a special force as Philautus advances the claims
of friendship. He has never failed Euphues in moments of mirth,
and neither does he fail him in time of sorrow. No sacrifice is too
great for Philautus! Lyly has created an incipient Palamon and Ar-
cite relationship, but he does not exploit the situation. Euphues
could have asked Philautus to make the sacrifice of which he speaks,
to sacrifice Lucilla to him. Instead, Euphues dissembles, pretending
that he loves Lucilla's handmaiden, Livia. Falling for the ruse,
Philautus welcomes Euphues as a fellow in wooing, although the
latter does utter a veiled warning—"take heed, my Philautus, that
thou thyself swallow not a gudgeon" (52)—which is lost on
Philautus. The effect which passion is working upon Euphues
becomes increasingly clear, as his concluding words in this encounter indicate: "Euphues consented willingly, smiling to himself
to see how he had brought Philautus into a fool's paradise" (53).

The third interlude, briefer than most, returns to the moralistic
form used in the first one: "Here you may see, gentlemen, the
falsehood in fellowship, the fraud in friendship, the painted sheath

with the leaden dagger, the fair words that make fools fain" (53). This interlude stresses the theme of appearance and reality which motivates much of the action in subsequent encounters. It is surely by design that Lyly stresses here the dissembling nature of Euphues, for Philautus must be convinced of Euphues's friendship before he departs with Ferardo, Lucilla's father. This interlude is important also because an irony emerges from Euphues's deception of Philautus. As he schemes his way into Lucilla's affections, he is actually plotting his own downfall. Precisely the same techniques of dissimulation that are being practiced upon Philautus by Euphues and Lucilla will be practiced on Euphues by Lucilla and Curio.

The fourth encounter involves Philautus, Euphues, Lucilla, and Livia, although Philautus leaves early in the scene and Livia makes her presence felt only at the close. At the prompting of Lucilla, Euphues resumes the discussion on love that he had abandoned in the third encounter. This time, possibly to advance his own suit, he begins by praising woman's modesty and constancy. His set piece is interrupted, however, by the arrival of Ferardo, who takes away Philautus, his prospective son-in-law, to settle a real estate transaction.

Left alone with Lucilla for the first time since his ardor has been awakened, Euphues, in proper Courtly fashion, presses his suit by pledging himself and his service to Lucilla. She is skeptical of easy victories, however, and decides to play the game of love with Euphues. First, she feigns anger. What, after all, does Euphues think that she is? How dare he repay her hospitality by attacking her constancy! She is quick to add, however, that she is not actually angry; but she is "in an agony; for who is she that will fret or fume with one that loveth her,—if this love to delude me be not dissembled?" (59).

Second, she grieves at the possibility of losing her reputation. Although Euphues is not the first to pursue her, she is still innocent in the "court of Cupid" (61). Then Lucilla moves rapidly through a series of temporary defenses, including (third) her father's reluctance to approve of Euphues; (fourth) the likelihood that Euphues, as a stranger, will travel on after obtaining her favors; (fifth) the fact that Euphues himself condemned beauty, calling it a poison; and, finally (sixth), that Euphues is motivated not by love but by lust.

Still unfinished, Lucilla launches into a mock-humble speech which stresses the inferior position of women:

Alas, we silly souls, which have neither wit to decipher the wiles of men nor wisdom to dissemble our affections [a lie, to be sure, since she has already dissembled with Philautus], neither craft to train in [to break in] young lovers [again a lie, for Euphues is breaking in at this very moment], neither courage to withstand their encounters, neither discretion to discern their doubling, neither hard hearts to reject their complaints—we, I say, are soon enticed, being by nature simple, and easily entangled, being apt to receive the impression of love (63).

Finally, after a last pretense in which she offers to be Euphues's *friend*, Lucilla capitulates on the condition that their love be kept secret.

The fourth interlude is occasioned by Ferardo's return and by the announcement of his daughter's forthcoming marriage to Philautus. A traditional feature of Roman comedy is thus introduced as a father stands between two young lovers, much as old Capulet stands between Romeo and Juliet. In *Euphues*, however, the Juliet is jaded, not the thirteen-year-old virgin of Shakespeare's play; thus Ferardo's reluctance to approve of Euphues produces an ironic effect.

The fifth encounter is unquestionably the most dramatic in the narrative. Ferardo, basing his approach on the ideals of motherhood, economic comfort, and the rest of the eternal parental verities, breaks the news to Lucilla of her forthcoming marriage to Philautus. She, however, will have none of it! Basing her refusal on the ideals of chastity, humility, and other eternal feminine verities, Lucilla breaks the news to Ferardo of her marriage to virginity. Besides, she adds anti-climactically, she will never marry a man whom she does not love. Sensing that Lucilla loves another, Ferardo pretends to agree that love is essential in marriage. He answers her spiritual objections by pointing to the sanctified nature of matrimony as described by the Patriarchs and Prophets. Finally, he agrees to accept any reasonable suitor whom Lucilla may propose, even though he be baseborn. Lucilla, suspecting a trap, nevertheless accepts her father's word and declares her love for Euphues.

Philautus reacts to this news by performing a series of emotional gymnastics. He begins by lamenting his own misfortune, then curses his false friend, Euphues, then proceeds to make excuses for both Euphues and Lucilla, and finally resolves to erase her from his memory. He will even forego revenge lest his old desire be re-awakened. The conflicting claims of love and friendship have here been settled in favor of love. But perhaps it should be regarded as lust, not love; for what has occurred is but prologue to a more disastrous disaffection which occurs later when Euphues plays the role of Philautus.

The fifth encounter is the emotional center of *Euphues*. Wit, which has been opposed to wisdom, has led to sorrow and anguish for Philautus; love, which is actually lust, for its motivation is entirely selfish, has destroyed friendship; willfulness rather than discipline, dissimulation rather than straightforwardness, passion rather than reason all work their insidious poison as Euphues and Lucilla, now passion's slaves, defy family and friends in pursuit of bodily delights. Nowhere in *Euphues* is the language more moving than in Philautus's lament:

Ah most dissembling wretch Euphues! O counterfeit companion! Couldst thou under the show of a steadfast friend cloak the malice of a mortal foe? Under the colour of simplicity shroud the image of deceit? Is thy Livia turned to my Lucilla, thy love to my lover, thy devotion to my saint? Is this the courtesy of Athens, the cavilling of scholars, the craft of Grecians? Couldst thou not remember, Philautus, that Greece is never without some wily Ulyssess, never void of some Sinon, never to seek of some deceitful shifter? (73)

The fifth interlude takes the form of an exchange of letters between Euphues and Philautus. Philautus writes that Euphues has made a poor bargain in sacrificing the true love of a friend for "the enticing looks of a lewd wench" (75). He also indicates that his failure to exact revenge should not be construed as weakness. Euphues is beyond reason by this point, however, and responds to Philautus's letter with contempt: "I am of this mind that both might and malice, deceit and treachery, all perjury, any impiety may lawfully be committed in love, which is lawless" (79). Euphues concludes his witty—and unwise—reply with insulting remarks about Philautus's lack of courage.

The poor bargain which Euphues has made is brought home to him in the sixth encounter. Lucilla, now in "love" with Curio, dissembles with Euphues as she has earlier dissembled with Philautus. When Euphues, returning from an absence of indeterminate length, rushes to the side of Lucilla, she rebuffs him with her disinterested reply: "Truely, Euphues, you have missed the cushion: for I was neither angry with your long absence, neither am I well pleased at your presence. The one gave me rather a good hope hereafter never to see you, the other giveth me a greater occasion to abhor you" (80).

Lyly displays here the spectacle of the disintegration of a personality totally diseased with lust. Reason has fled to brutish beasts, and Lucilla cites her own irrationality as she attempts to explain her situation: "I have chosen one (I must needs confess) neither to be compared to Philautus in wealth, nor to thee in wit, neither in birth to the worst of you both. I think God gave it me for a just plague for renouncing Philautus and choosing thee; and sithence I am an ensample to all women of lightness, I am like also to be a mirror to them all of unhappiness. Which ill luck I must take by so much the more patiently, by how much the more I acknowledge myself to have deserved it worthily" (81-82).

Lucilla serves as an object lesson in the ethical universe of *Euphues*. Having devoted herself to self-gratifying pleasure, she now begins the decline which will ultimately result in her total degeneration (cf. p. 47). The witlessness of her present decision to overthrow Euphues in favor of Curio is manifested in the opening sentence of the passage just quoted. She has traded prestige and security and received nothing in return—she does not even mention love. Instead, she has adopted the pose of the fallen woman; she glories in self-recrimination and guilt; and, aware of her own moral failings, she still refuses to seek redemption. The present state of her moral depravity is suggested also by the condition of her new lover: " . . . in body deformed, in mind foolish, an innocent born, a beggar by misfortune" (83). Curio is indeed a curiosity, a blend of all that Lucilla would ordinarily detest—physical and mental deformity coupled with poverty; and he is hardly the kind of man a reasonable woman would seek to love. In this way Lyly suggests the lengths to which a woman will go in pursuit of forbidden fruit. The destructive effects of the undisciplined life are evident.

Euphues is able at last to recognize the poor bargain he has made; and, a confirmed anti-feminist, he leaves Lucilla. His education through experience is just beginning, however, for, just as he has gone to extremes in his pursuit of Lucilla, he now goes to extremes in his renunciation of her. It is not enough for Euphues to condemn Lucilla; he must also condemn all women. As a result of his reaction, the sixth interlude takes the form of Euphues's condemnation of women. Euphues rallies many of the traditional Medieval misogynistic arguments that remained alive in the Renaissance. Unlike men, who are "true, faithful, zealous, constant," women are noted for "falsehood, jealousy, inconstancy" (84). They have "tasted of the infection of the serpent and will be corrosives" (84). With this allusion to the *Eva rediva* theme, and with Euphues's realization that a fair exterior frequently hides a foul interior, he announces his retirement from the world. Books will now be his mistress; the study, his court.

The seventh, and last, encounter in *Euphues* is between Lucilla and Ferardo. The prodigal-son motif, with which the narrative began, is transformed into the prodigal-daughter one. Ferardo appeals to his daughter to return to reason, but she will have none of it. There is no forgiveness and reconciliation, as one expects in a prodigal-son story. Instead, Lucilla breaks her father's heart, and Ferardo dies shortly thereafter. Lucilla now disappears from the narrative, and her subsequent history is neglected until Lyly in *Euphues and His England* briefly mentions her ill-fated end.

There is, however, a reconciliation between Euphues and Philautus. In the seventh interlude, which takes the form of narrative summation, the two former friends renew their friendship. Philautus has become so enamored of courtly life that he desires to remain in Naples, and Euphues returns alone to Athens. He remains concerned about Philautus's future, for to Euphues Naples stands for evil. Furthermore, Philautus has not forsworn the romantic life, a dangerous proclivity which prompts Euphues to compose for his friend a "cooling card." "A Cooling Card for Philautus and All Fond Lovers" is Euphues's "remedy . . . for love" (91). A lengthy letter, it reemphasizes a number of themes and attitudes which have appeared in *Euphues*. Among the more important are: (1) misogynism—"deluded by women, the gate to perdition" (93); (2) asceticism—"confer all thy study, all thy time, all thy treasure to the attaining of the sacred and sincere knowledge of divinity; by this mayest thou bridle thine incontinency, rein thine affections, restrain thy lust" (100); (3) the *vanitas vanitatum* theme—"Here shalt thou behold as it were in a glass that all the glory of man is as the grass, that all things under heaven are but vain, that our life is but a shadow, a warfare, a pilgrimage, a vapour, a bubble, a blast" (100); and (4) Arcadianism—"Go into the country. Look to thy grounds, yoke thine oxen, follow thy plough, graft thy trees, behold thy cattle, and devise with thyself how the increase of them may increase thy profit" (101).[6]

Furthermore, as Euphues explains, the nature of women militates against edifying relationships. It is "folly to show wit to women which are neither able nor willing to receive fruit thereof" (100). After all, what else can be expected from creatures whose nature "is grounded only upon extremities" (102) and who misrepresent themselves by using cosmetics (103-104)? But even as he condemns women, Euphues is conscious of their fatal attraction; and, unconsciously perhaps, he speaks of them in the traditional language of love: "idleness is . . . the first shaft that Cupid shooteth into the hot liver of a heedless lover" (98). Euphues also shows an acute awareness of the problem created by a society that encourages young men to pursue young girls at the risk of being ostracized by their peers for failure to do so. " 'If I refuse their courtesy I shall be accounted a meacock, a milksop, taunted and retaunted with check and checkmate, flouted and reflouted with intolerable glee' " (95).

Euphues ends his "Cooling Card" with an apology to all "honest matrons" whom he exempts from criticism. This section of the narrative, entitled "To the Grave Matrons, and Honest Maidens of Italy" (107-110), serves as a palinode to the "Cooling Card" and is brief and unexceptional. It is followed, however, by a transition paragraph which informs the reader of Euphues's new interest in education, and thus prepares for the lengthy section entitled "Euphues and His Ephebus"[7] (111-142).

Whereas the fifth encounter is the emotional core of *Euphues*, the Ephebus episode is the thematic center in that wit is now redeemed. Or, as Lyly states, "And calling to mind his [Euphues's] former looseness and how in his youth he had misspent his time, he thought to give a caveat to all parents how they might bring their children up in virtue, and a commandment to all youth how they should frame themselves to their father's instructions; in the which is plainly to be seen what wit can and will do if it be well employed" (110). Although wit has been played off against wisdom consistently throughout *Euphues*, Lyly now mitigates the contrast so that the one no longer excludes the other. In fact, wit now becomes the handmaiden of wisdom. Lyly also informs the reader at this point that his theme henceforth will be reason, not love. The Ephebus section introduces Euphues's attempts to establish his educational Utopia.[8] He begins by placing a premium on experience as a teacher: "He that hath been burned knoweth the force of the fire, he that hath been stung remembereth the smart of the scorpion, he that hath endured the brunts of fancy knoweth best how to eschew the broils of affection" (111-112). Then he announces his intentions of laying down rules so absolute that nothing further need be added for the perfection of children. The rules, such as they are, reveal no revolutionary reforms; in fact, they recapitulate many of the points made in the opening speech of Eubulus: a child must be trueborn, and no bastard (114-115). The three essential qualities of any child are nature, discipline, and use. By "nature" Euphues means wit: "For nature without discipline is of small force, and discipline without nature more feeble; if exercise or study be void of any of these it availeth nothing" (115). And, he then says, "if there be any one that deemeth wit not necessary to the obtaining of wisdom . . . , he is an heretic" (115). It is, finally, education, as Eubulus argued, that "altereth nature" for either good or evil.

The greater part of "Euphues and His Ephebus" is devoted to a section entitled "Of the Education of Youth" (116-142), which Lyly summarizes thus:

The sum of all, wherewith I would have my Ephebus endued and how I would have him instructed, shall briefly appear in this following: first, that he be of honest parents, nursed of his mother, brought up in such a place as is incorrupt both for the air and manners, with such a person as is undefiled, of great zeal, of profound knowledge, of absolute perfection; that he be instructed in philosophy, whereby he may attain learning, and have in all sciences a smack, whereby he may readily dispute of anything; that his body be kept in his pure strength by honest exercise, his wit and memory by diligent study; that he abandon all allurements of vice and continually incline to virtue. Which if it shall, as it may, come to pass, then do I hope that if ever Plato's commonweal shall flourish that my Ephebus shall be a citizen, that if Aristotle find any happy man it will be my child, if Tully confess any to be an absolute orator it will be my young youth. (139-140)

There is in this educational treatise much about traditional educational theory but little about educational reform. As is fitting, since most of the content comes from Plutarch, the general aim of this educational system is to impart such Classical values as decorum and eloquence; but almost nothing is said about the Humanist reforms which were at that time sweeping England. Euphues does attack the speculative life, but his doing so is unfortunate since he later embraces it himself. Outside of this attack, and a few anti-Papist remarks, nothing in this educational treatise makes it representative of its time. It is ironic, of course, that Euphues, who at the beginning was described by Eubulus as a young man lacking both sobriety and discipline, now champions these very virtues.

The circle has almost come full round, and Lyly is just about where he started. The virtues of temperance and decorum, virtues attained only in the school of experience, are being proclaimed by age to youth; but not, however, until Euphues assumes the occupation of Eubulus is the return complete. That moment occurs in the following interlude, one which takes the form of the author's summary of the important events in the life of the protagonist. In spite of what Euphues has said earlier about the evil of the contemplative life, he now embraces it. After some time spent as a Public Reader in the University, Euphues decides that his pursuits are vain, that only Christ is worth pursuing. Accordingly, he bids goodby to Aristotle, Cicero, and Ovid in order to devote his full attention to Divine Scripture.

Subsequent to Euphues's "conversion" is his desire that all men similarly find the true path, and in a letter entitled "Euphues to the Gentlemen Scholars in Athens" (145-146) he tries to impress upon his fellow scholars the fact that life is a "pilgrimage" (146) and that "vain is philosophy, vain is physic, vain is law, vain is all learning without the taste of divine knowledge" (146). In order to develop his contention, Euphues presents for the edification of his fellows a dialogue which he held with a heretic. This dialogue, entitled "Euphues and Atheos," is a brief summation of the pilgrimage which Euphues has undertaken in the narrative. In short, Atheos experiences a spiritual conversion which counterpoints that of Euphues.[9] Most important of all, however, is that *wit* has disappeared from the reformed Euphues's vocabulary. In the conversation with Eubulus at the start of the narrative, the word appeared eleven times in twelve pages; here it does not appear even once in fifteen pages. At the beginning of *Euphues*, Lyly contrasted wit and wisdom; and he was obviously favoring wisdom. Later in the book, however, wit takes on new meaning so that it can serve as the handmaiden of wisdom; but it no longer appears to be important. This change can be explained by the fact that *wisdom*, as will be shown, now assumes a new meaning, one which plants it squarely in this world rather than in the next.

With the exception of the postscript, *Euphues* concludes with "Certain Letters Writ by Euphues to His Friends" (163-183), none over five pages in length, which cover a multitude of topics.[10] There are seven letters (perhaps to parallel the seven encounters?), the first of which is addressed to Philautus (163-168). This letter has as its theme the dispraise of courtly life. Euphues criticizes Philautus's courtly life and warns him that if he desires to be saved, he must "contemn the world, embrace Christ, leave the court, follow thy study, prefer holiness before honour, honesty before promotion, religion and uprightness of life before the overlashing desires of the flesh" (167). In the course of this letter Euphues again uses the words *wit* and *wisdom*, but their meanings have shifted: "Aristotle with all his wit, all men with all their wisdom have and shall perish and turn to dust" (165). In the course of his pilgrimage Euphues has come to realize a new meaning, a new level of existence, where neither wit nor wisdom is sufficient unless each is accompanied by faith. For Euphues, both wit and wisdom now play a role subservient to faith. This change, then, explains why the word *wit* does not appear in the dialogue with Atheos—it is no longer relevant!

The second and third letters, "Euphues to Eubulus" and "Euphues to Philautus," form an effective contrast in that the former concerns the death of a young, innocent girl and the latter the death of a jaded, not-so-innocent Lucilla. The second letter permits Lyly to meditate on the *de Contemptu Mundi* theme, wherein he sounds amazingly like Dr. Johnson: "In life there is nothing sweet, in death nothing sour" (168).

The third letter brings to a close the story of Lucilla, who, like Cressida before her, dies a beggar in the streets. Her terrible end is

intended, of course, to be a sign of God's divine providence—an
evil end to an evil life. And Euphues is quick to take advantage of
the lesson which Lucilla instances, for he writes to Philautus that
"whoso liveth in the court shall die in the straw" (170).

The fourth letter, which urges Botonio to "take his exile patiently," is an abridged translation of Plutarch's *De Exilio,* and may have
provided Shakespeare with a hint for Gaunt's speech to his exiled
son in *Richard II* (I.iii.275-293). Peter Ure argues that "Shakespeare
must recently have read or re-read Lyly's letter . . . that gave him
the idea for the scene in which the sage father offers Plutarchan
consolations to the exiled son."[11]

The fifth letter, "Euphues to a young gentleman in Athens
named Alcius . . ." (175-178), discusses the nature of true nobility. In
this letter Lyly espouses the Renaissance, Humanist notion that
gentlemen are made, not born: "It is not the descent of birth but
the consent of conditions that maketh gentlemen, neither great
manors but good manners that express the true image of dignity"
(176).

The sixth letter, "Livia, from the Emperor's court, to Euphues at
Athens" (178-179), is, like the first, in dispraise of courtly life. The
problem in dispraising court life is that the writer is implicitly condemning courtly personages, including the queen, as well as
manners and mores. In order to remove the onus from himself, Lyly
praises the queen at the same time that he condemns her court.
Livia writes that, although the empress tries her hardest to inculcate
a sense of values in her people, no one pays attention to her: "The
Empress keepeth her estate royal and·her maidens will not leese an
inch of their honour; she endeavoureth to set down good laws and
they to break them, she warneth them of excess and they study to
exceed, she saith that decent attire is good though it be not costly
and they swear unless it be dear it is not comely" (179).

The seventh, and last, letter, "Euphues to his friend Livia" (180-
183), continues the dispraise of courtly life, but adds little to what
has already been said. Euphues commends Livia for her honest
report of conditions at court, applauds her decision to retire to country life, laments over Philautus's vain pursuits, and concludes by an-
nouncing Euphues's intention to travel to England where he has
"heard of a woman that in all qualities excelleth any man" (183). In
view of this obvious allusion to Queen Elizabeth, it is unlikely that

"the Empress" of the last letter is meant to figure Elizabeth.[12]
With this letter, *Euphues, the Anatomy of Wit* draws to a close.
All that is left is for Euphues to announce that the second part of
the narrative will shortly be forthcoming. The "Postscript," "To My
Very Good Friends the Gentlemen Scholars of Oxford" (184-186),
first appeared in the second edition; and thereafter it was transferred in all editions to the front of the book.
The ironic thrust of the narrative has been driven home. Outcome has, indeed, proved contrary to expectation! Euphues, the
youthful opportunist who sought courtly preferment and passionate
delights, now embraces a life of solitude. Euphues's journey
through life has reinforced Eubulus's advice that to be in society is
to be of society, and that the latter implies, for the perceptive man
at least, a kind of spiritual death. Euphues has at last seen the
morality of the court for what it really is—at best, frivolous; at
worst, vicious. His journey has answered, ironically, the very question with which he began his journey: "will you [Eubulus] con-
clude, as it were *ex consequenti*, that whosoever arriveth here shall
be enticed to folly and, being enticed, of force shall be entangled?"
(22).

II Euphues and His England

As has been noted, *Euphues and His England* is longer, more
dramatic, and generally superior to *Euphues, the Anatomy of Wit*.
Much of the moralizing has been replaced by dialogue and encounter; therefore, the narrative reads less like a moral treatise and
more like a novel. The structure, particularly, marks an advance in
Lyly's artistry. The encounter-interlude structure which served for
Euphues is replaced by a less episodic technique. The encounters
are still present, but they are no longer interrupted by lengthy
moralizing reflections. Instead, Lyly omits the homilies, shortens
the interludes to a page or two, and generally uses them to advance
theme or plot.
It is curious that G. K. Hunter chose not to work out a five-act
structure for *Euphues and His England*, for the work falls into five
parts more readily than its predecessor:

I. Euphues and Philautus travel together to London where they
separate (205-316).

II.   Philautus unsuccessfully courts Camilla (316-362).
III. Euphues and Philautus are reconciled (362-377).
IV. After the symposium, Euphues and Philautus separate again (377-414).
V.   Exchange of letters between Euphues (in Athens), Flavia and Philautus (both in London) (415-462).

The first part introduces Camilla, whom Philautus courts in the second part, only to see the folly of his ways and resume his friendship with Euphues in the third part. The fourth part repeats, inversely, the first one as Euphues and Philautus separate a second time. The fifth is actually a long postscript and serves as a coda for both *Euphues* and *Euphues and His England*.

Perhaps because the work was dedicated to Lord Oxford, whose taste for ladies of fashion was notorious, or perhaps because he discovered that commercial success was pleasant, Lyly devotes most of *Euphues and His England* to love and to Philautus. Philautus is the protagonist, even though Euphues remains the title character; and among the various themes none is handled with the same tenaciousness as is love. Love causes Euphues and Philautus to separate (as it did in *Euphues*); love occupies the entire "second act" during which Philautus unsuccessfully woos Camilla; disappointment in love causes Philautus and Euphues to repair their friendship (as it did also in *Euphues*); love, in in the form of the symposium, occupies all of the "fourth act"; and, finally, love prompts the exchange of letters in the "last act."

In devoting *Euphues and His England* to love and ladies, Lyly may have been reacting to courtly criticism. He says in the "Epistle Dedicatory" that with his first book he was "stricken into disgrace" (196). Thus regarded, *Euphues and His England* becomes a recantation of all the nasty things that Lyly had to say about ladies in *Euphues;* but authors' protests ought not to be taken too seriously.

Better evidence that Lyly was courting public approval is to be found in "To the Ladies and Gentlewomen of England John Lyly Wisheth What They Would" (199-202). Here the major theme of the work is announced—"divers questions and quirks of love"—as well as the basic technique, "These discourses I have not clapt in a cluster . . . I have sowed them here and there" (199). The book will not be a sustained discussion of love; it will be a narrative dealing with many different topics; and love will be its focal point. Finally, the tone, which is strikingly different from its predecessor, is sounded: "Euphues had rather be shut in a lady's casket than open in a scholar's study" (200). As Feuillerat noted, in *Euphues and His England* Lyly appeals to the courtly frivolity against which he inveighed in *Euphues*.[13]

Lyly defends his new approach, basing his defense on a principle of decorum: "The old hermit will have his talk savour of his cell; the old courtier, his love taste of Saturn [dull, leaden]; yet the last lover may haply come somewhat near Jupiter [joyful, zestful]" (204). Obviously, Lyly was sensitive to the criticism leveled against *Euphues;* and he selected his theme and tone in *Euphues and His England* with an eye to public approval. Yet he sounds uncertain of his ability to handle the theme of love, almost a little frightened of its implications.

The narrative proper begins with a brief introduction which establishes the date of Euphues's voyage to England, and it is followed by the first encounter between Euphues and Philautus (205-230). This encounter, however, is more complex than any in *Euphues.* Here is a tale within a tale within a tale, as Euphues tells a story about Callimachus, who tells a story about a hermit. Actually, *Euphues and His England* begins much the same way as *Euphues* begins. In both, a lesson is used to instigate action; in both, the lesson is lost on the listener; in both, the lesson occupies a considerable portion of the narrative. The similarity serves, however, to emphasize the difference in methods of narration in the two works. In *Euphues* the lesson of Eubulus quickly became tedious, but in *Euphues and His England* the shifting point of view adds richness to the fabric of the narrative.

To pass the time on the voyage to London, Euphues proposes to tell a story he has heard from a hermit; but Philautus, still smarting from the pangs of disappointed love, asks instead for an elegy from Ovid. Undaunted, Euphues launches into the story of Cassandra and Callimachus (207-225). Callimachus, disappointed by his father's legacy of platitudes, sets out to make his fortune; and he immediately encounters a hermit who just happens to be his uncle who is holding ten thousand pounds in trust for him. The uncle, who closely resembles Eubulus, volunteers to tell a tale of his own.

The uncle tells an autobiographical story about twins who,

though identical in appearance, are opposed in temperament. The prodigal twin, who turns out to be the uncle, when faced with a legacy of two bags, one filled with gold, the other with paper, selects the former and squanders the money in riotous living. Fourteen years of luxurious travel all but destroy his body and soul; in penance, he retires from the world. The wise brother, Cassandra, remains at home and prospers. At the conclusion of his story, the hermit summarizes the dangers of travel; but Callimachus, a callow youth, will not profit from the voice of experience. Arguing that no one should generalize on the basis of one example, Callimachus sets off and suffers the identical fate the hermit prophesied. Thoroughly chastened, Callimachus returns home, and the hermit gives him his inheritance.

The relevance of the double story, not readily apparent, becomes clear as Euphues explains to Philautus why he has been subjected to it: both Callimachus and the hermit were ill prepared to travel. Both sought the wrong things, for, as Euphues explains, ". . . either never to travel, or so to travel as although the purse be weakened the mind may be strengthened. For not he that hath seen most countries is most to be esteemed, but he that learned best conditions; for not so much is the situation of the places to be noted as the virtues of the persons . . . our travellers . . . go either for gain and return without knowledge, or for fashion sake and come home without piety" (225-226).

In this way, then, Euphues impresses his point upon Philautus and does so without resorting to sermons. The Eubulus episode with which *Euphues* began is here transferred into material appropriate to narrative. Whereas Eubulus preached a *sermon*, Euphues and Callimachus *narrate* stories. Furthermore, they are stories of conflict; and the narrative itself is more dramatic. This section concludes with Euphues's description of England based on Caesar's *Gallic Wars*. Here Lyly is undoubtedly poking fun at travel literature and at the gross inaccuracies which it fostered, for better and more accurate descriptions of England than Caesar's were available to him.

Although the opening of *Euphues and His England* is far superior to the opening of *Euphues*, Philautus is not suitably impressed. He tells Euphues, "The beginning I have forgotten, the middle I understand not, and the end hangeth not together" (228-229). After eight weeks at sea, Euphues and Philautus land at Dover and make their way to London; but they pause at Canterbury, the probable birthplace of John Lyly (230-232). On the road to London, Euphues and Philautus encounter Fides, a onetime courtier under Henry VIII. Curious about the queen who rules in England, Euphues questions Fides, who, though reluctant, suggests that Elizabeth is a personage not to be scrutinized too closely: "Things above us are not for us, and therefore are princes placed under the gods, that they should not see what they do, and we under princes, that we might not inquire what they do" (238-239).

After Fides's description of the monarchy, based on the commonplace of the beehive, he delivers himself of a tale which is actually a capsule version of *Euphues* (247-257); but parts of the tale may be autobiographical. Like Lyly—or Euphues—Fides has been born of good parents; is not inferior in wit to many; has sought a life at court, where he became fast friends with a gentleman; and has aspired toward courtly preferment. After a description of the perfect courtier, Fides proceeds to describe his unrequited love for a lady he calls Iffida. Although the description interests Philautus, it puts Euphues to sleep; and Fides postpones the rest of his tale to the following day.

A short interruption by the author (257-258) serves not only to pass the night but also to clarify his position as a writer of love stories. Lyly directly addresses the reader: "In the discourse of this love it may seem I have taken a new course" (257), thus distinguishing *Euphues and His England* from its predecessor. Lyly defends his new approach, with a touch of irony, on the grounds of popular appeal: "And to that pass it is come that they make an art of that which was wont to be thought natural" (258).

The last part of Fides's tale (259-285) is devoted to "questions of love," set topics which exercise the ingenuity of the participants. The "questions" go back to Boccaccio, but they found their most popular outlet, especially in England, in Baldassare Castiglione's *The Courtier*.[14] The first question—who is most desirable, a fair fool, a witty wanton, or a crooked saint—is decided by Fides in favor of the witty wanton; for what a man does not know will not hurt him. The second question—who is most desirable, a man with gifts of the body, a man with a quick wit, or a man with great wealth—is answered, after much evasion, by Iffida in favor of the wealthy man; for "beauty without riches goeth a begging, and wit without wealth cheapeneth [bargains for] all things in the Fair but buyeth nothing" (276).

The questions of love are momentarily set aside while Fides describes his lovesickness, a description which is merely a prologue to Iffida's reaction when she hears of the death of her lover, Thirsus. She first falls into a frenzy, then suffers a hot pestilent fever, and finally dies. Her death occasions Fides's definition of love:

You see what Love is—begun with grief, continued with sorrow, ended with death; a pain full of pleasure, a joy replenished with misery, a Heaven, a Hell, a God, a Devil, and what not, that either hath in it solace or sorrow; where the days are spent in thoughts, the nights in dreams, both in danger; either beguiling us of that we had, or promising us that we had not; full of jealousy without cause, and void of fear when there is cause; and so many inconveniences hanging upon it as to reckon them all were infinite, and to taste but one of them intolerable.

Yet in these days it is thought the signs of a good wit and the only virtue peculiar to a courtier. For love they say is in young gentlemen; in clowns it is lust, in old men dotage; when it is in all men madness. (285)

At this point in the narrative, Lyly rescues Euphues and Philautus from Fides and returns them to the road to London. Euphues delivers a sermon to Philautus on the dangers of women, but the incurably romantic Philautus has by now become surfeited with all the advice he has received of late. But, after he and Euphues arrive at the house of Camilla, Philautus is immediately smitten with love for the lady. He is initally confused by the experience: "What strange fits be these, Philautus, that burn thee with such a heat that thou shakest for cold, and all thy body in a shivering sweat, in a flaming ice, melteth like wax and hardeneth like the adament? Is it love? Then would it were death!" (292). Philautus is further upset because he is an Italian, and so considered vicious by the virtuous English. In defense, he cries out: "An Englishman has three qualities: he can suffer no partner in his love, no stranger to be his equal, nor to be dared by any" (297).

The author again intervenes, this time to bring Euphues to Philautus so that their friendship can be threatened a second time. The cause is, of course, love; but now Euphues espouses the cause of women while Philautus chastises them, thereby reversing the roles

they enact in *Euphues*. In Philautus's description of his love symptoms, the language is restricted to Petrarchan terms of natural
phenomenon—burn, shiver, heat, cold—but now it modulates into
the courtly language of the religion of love, as ecclesiastical terms
such as "heresy" and "penance" recall both Medieval Courts of
Love and *The Courtier*. To reinforce his new attitude toward women, Euphues declares that his "Cooling Card" was rash and
peremptory.

Philautus is disturbed by Euphues's recantation and by what he
considers to be hypocrisy. Insulted by Philautus's charges, Euphues
accuses him of being a false friend and leaves, just as Philautus
leaves in *Euphues*. History has repeated itself, and it is about to
repeat itself again as the author returns Philautus to Camilla. He
woos her at a masked ball (as in *Much Ado About Nothing*) but
loses her to another suitor (as in *Euphues*). Now Philautus's mood
ranges from black despair at the start to new hopefulness at the end.
The effect of passion, however, is ultimately to distort his sense of
values, and he reveals his familiarity with Machiavelli's *The Prince*:
"In the ruling of empires there is required as great policy as
prowess; in governing an estate close cruelty doth more good than
open clemency; for the obtaining of a kingdom as well mischief as
mercy is to be practised. . . . Nor he that is in love be curious what
means he ought to use, but ready to attempt any" (322).[15] Even
though fully aware of the wickedness that he is advocating,
Philautus is "fully resolved either by art to win her love or by
despair to lose mine own life" (323). He seeks, therefore, the aid of
a fellow Italian, Psellus, who will do anything for money.

After a brief authorial comment about the evils to which love can
drive an otherwise good man, Philautus asks Psellus to assist him in
securing the affections of Camilla. Although competent in the black
arts, Psellus replies that no man can encroach on the domain of the
gods: "Do you think, gentleman, that the mind being created of
God can be ruled by man or that anyone can move the heart but He
that made the heart?" (329). Like Dipsas, the enchantress in *Endimion*, Psellus denies the efficacy of magic in affairs of the heart.
Love carries a religious sanction; it is an inviolable contract: "Love
dwelleth in the mind, in the will, and in the hearts, which neither
conjurer can alter nor physic. . . . The will is placed in the soul.
And who can enter there, but He that created the soul?" (335). This

comment prompts one from the author upon the state to which men have reduced love. The original lovers, Adam and Eve, used no deception. Only postlapsarian man is attracted by duplicity, and thus man has corrupted the simplicity of true love based on faith and has substituted for it an elaborate display of appearance (338-339).

The following thirty-eight pages of *Euphues and His England* are divided into thirty-two short sections; none is over four pages in length, and most are in the form of epistles or authorial insertions. The rest are love encounters between Philautus and Camilla. Because of the brevity of the sections, this part of the book tends to move very swiftly.

Momentarily overcoming his fear that his love for Camilla may be made public, Philautus writes her a love letter. The letter is hidden in a pomegranate which Camilla receives when she complains of stomach trouble. After Philautus leaves, Camilla discovers the letter but is not pleased. Her reply to Philautus, hidden in her edition of Petrarch, advises him to look elsewhere. When Philautus returns, Camilla asks him to explicate a verse in her Petrarch; and she then shows him her letter. Although he is at first discouraged, Philautus convinces himself that if Camilla were not interested in him, she would not have taken the time to write the letter (she wrote, actually, so that Philautus would not be encouraged by her silence).

When Philautus writes a second letter, also secreted in Camilla's Petrarch, she becomes furious and threatens to expose him if he persists. And he does!—but not until after he "tare his hair, rent his clothes, and fell from the passions of a lover to the pangs of frenzy" (360). Camilla ultimately ends the exchange of letters, and Philautus desists in his suit. At last Philautus comes to realize that true friendship is to be more highly prized than love, a lesson learned by Euphues in *The Anatomy of Wit*.

An exchange of letters follows between Philautus and Euphues which balances the previous exchange between Philautus and Camilla. Twice Philautus writes and apologizes for his break with Euphues; twice Euphues doubts Philautus's sincerity and postpones the reconciliation. Finally, in order to demonstrate his sincerity, Philautus proclaims his reformation, calling upon God as his witness. This time Philautus's letter convinces Euphues, and the reconciliation is effected. The author at this point interrupts with a "question of love" of his own, viz., whether there is in men an art of love or whether it breeds in them, by sight, hearing, etc.

Euphues advises Philautus that love at first sight is no basis for a lasting relationship, and he urges Philautus to forget Camilla and to pursue Frances. Philautus agrees but fears that in chasing two women, he will catch neither; but he is assured by Euphues that "there cometh greater delight in the hunting than in the eating" (379). Philautus, however, likes to have the game in his dish at night, and he will not be persuaded that talking, eating, and laughing with ladies are as agreeable as loving them. When Euphues argues that men can enjoy flowers without picking them and that it is more enjoyable to communicate with women on the spiritual level through discourse than on the physical level through bestial intercourse, Philautus labels this argument as "heresy" (380).

This debate over the two kinds of love, spiritual and physical, is derived in part from Plutarch's essay on love which appears in Book IV of Castiglione's *The Courtier;* and the argument reaches its peak as Euphues argues, along Neoplatonic lines, that the eye and the ear cooperate in building a chaste love in heavenly meditations, rather than in temporal actions. But Euphues's bubble is neatly burst by Philautus, who contemptuously replies that deaf-and-dumb persons also love. The author throws his support to Philautus when he says, "The end of love is the full fruition of the party beloved, at all times and in all places" (382).

Following this authorial comment, Flavia proposes that the guests choose sides—Surius against Camilla, Philautus against Frances, Martius against Flavia—and discuss questions of love (in the tradition of Giovanni Boccaccio's *Filocolo,* Baldassare Castiglione's *The Courtier,* and Edmund Tylney's *Flower of Friendship*). The following section (386-406) constitutes Lyly's most prolonged and serious meditation on the subject of love to be found anywhere in his writings.

Question one: Surius asks Camilla how she would answer a man who offered her his service, but she evades the question by replying that she would admit his service if he were constant. The real issue behind this initial debate, however, has to do with the cause of love; that is, whether love resides in the beloved or in the eye of the beholder. Camilla argues for the former, but she cautions that such love is often merely lust. Surius argues that love is bred by the eyes and the ears. Thus for Surius, a deaf-and-dumb woman might be loved by a man. Since neither participant is willing to concede, Flavia cuts short the debate and engages Martius in a debate of her own.

Question two: Flavia asks Martius whether young men and women should be permitted to meet since such meetings are a source of temptation. Martius argues that the love that might result from such a meeting is to be preferred to the madness (melancholy) that would result from forced separation. Surius, an impatient listener, suddenly blurts out his support of Martius's position, and Flavia again cuts short the discussion.

Question three: Philautus asks Frances which is more important in love, secrecy or constancy. She replies that love requires three qualities: affection, secrecy, and constancy. The argument wavers, but no final resolution is reached. When Flavia calls upon Euphues to render his verdict, he replies that although he knows nothing about the laws of love, he does know something about the dangers of love which praises beauty at the expense of virtue. All such love he would discourage by whatever means possible. Then Euphues offers his definition of love: "True and virtuous love is to be grounded upon time, reason, favour, and virtue. Time, to make trial . . . Reason, that all his doings . . . flow [not] from a mind inflamed with lust . . . Favour, to delight his eyes . . . Virtue, to allure the soul . . ." (406). Following this definition Euphues renders his verdict: Surius is wrong, for love comes from both the man and the woman. Flavia's question is pointless, for lovers will always find a way to meet. Philautus's question is poor, for both secrecy and constancy are necessary. English logic thus vanquishes Continental sophistication!

This verdict ends the discussion of the questions of love, and the group disperses for the night. The pace of the narrative accelerates as the following ten pages return to the earlier format of short one- or two-page episodes. The first of these takes the form of Camilla's lament. Deeply in love with Surius, Camilla, frying in the flames of love, is uncertain whether she should reveal her love; for she fears that Surius may reject her. This episode is quickly concluded by the author's comment that no one is safe from love's agony.

Then Lyly returns to Euphues and Philautus, and he permits Euphues to chide his friend for fickleness in now loving Frances. Philautus, however, has profited from his experiences in love; he admits that "if ever I kill myself for love it shall be with a sigh, not with a sword" (410). When letters from Athens arrive requiring Euphues's return, Philautus, too much in love to leave Frances, declines to accompany him. Euphues's departure occupies three pages and quite some time; he first says goodby to his friends, Flavia, Surius, Camilla, and Frances; then to Fides, whom he encounters on the road to Dover; and, finally, to Philautus, who accompanies him as far as the ship. From Athens [Oxford?], Euphues writes his famous "Glass for Europe" (417-448).[16] After an introductory letter to Livia and a dedication "To the ladies and gentlewomen of Italy" (415-416), Euphues announces that his "Glass" is to be a corrective for Italian women wherein they can see reflected their vice and the virtue of English women. In the first part of "Glass for Europe" (417-426), Euphues offers a physical description of England, mainly London, followed by descriptions of institutions, diet, dress, law, four-footed animals, minerals, manners, the court, and the government, including Lord Burleigh. In the second part (427-432), which is devoted to moralizing, Euphues praises the virtues of Englishwomen at the expense of their Italian counterparts, who prefer Ariosto and Petrarch to Holy Scripture.

The third part (432-448) is an elaborate tribute to Queen Elizabeth. After a brief historical sketch which covers the War of the Roses, Euphues cites the marriage of Henry VII and Elizabeth of York as divinely ordained. The reigns of Edward and Mary are touched upon, and the remainder of the "Glass" is devoted to Elizabeth. Her outstanding qualities, Euphues repeats time after time, are mercy and justice. Since she is a virgin, Euphues is able to heap lavish praise upon her chastity, one of his favorite topics. National security, however, demanded an heir; and Euphues is more than willing to sacrifice the royal virginity for the objective. After comparing Elizabeth's intellectual accomplishments with those of other famous women, Lyly concludes this section with "Jovis Elizabeth," a Latin poem praising England's majesty.

Euphues and His England ends with a return to the friendship theme with which it began. Realizing that matters in England are "but rawly left" (449), Lyly says that he will write about Philautus's letters from London. When Philautus reports not only that Camilla and Surius have wed but also that he and Frances have become engaged, the announcement triggers a characteristic reaction as Euphues writes a letter to Philautus about the duties of husbands. Yet the advice which comes so easily to Euphues seems cold comfort when contrasted to Philautus's happiness. In fact, the last view presented of the two friends shows Philautus enjoying his new wife in London while Euphues, tormented in body and grieved in mind, isolates himself in the mountains of Silixsedra. The moral seems clear: Euphues, in spite of his clear-sighted, moral approach to the art of living, has become the final object of Lyly's irony—love in isolation is cold comfort indeed!

CHAPTER 3

Early Plays

JOHN Lyly's plays occupy a pivotal position in the history of English dramatic comedy. At the same time, he looks back to the allegorical drama of the fifteenth and sixteenth centuries, and he looks forward to the romantic comedy of the 1590's and to the romances of the early seventeenth century. His debt to the past is, however, difficult to estimate. Usually, he is considered to be a late manifestation of the spirit of allegory which dominated the English morality play; but Lyly's indebtedness to the morality drama is actually slight. Like morality plays, Lyly's comedies are heavily moralistic; and a thematic similarity certainly exists between *Midas* and *All for Money* (1577). But the morality plays which were closest to Lyly in point of time, the "intermediate" moralities of the sixteenth century, stress a set of motives generally foreign to Lyly.[1]

Lyly's comedies illustrate the search for love and nobility and are set amid an atmosphere of adventure and romance, but the "intermediate" moralities stress the craving for wealth and power and the effect that lust creates in a spiritually diseased personality. Furthermore, the "intermediate" moralities concentrate on bourgeois characters and rely heavily on scurrility and low humor. Lyly's comedies, however, concentrate on lofty personages, such as Alexander the Great and Midas, and generally eschew scurrility and low humor. On the occasions when the protagonists are lowborn, as in *Gallathea* and *Loves Metamorphosis*, Lyly elevates them by association with outstanding mythological personages. In short, "intermediate" moralities such as *The Tide Tarrieth No Man* (1576), *The Longer Thou Liveth* (1558-1569), *The More Fool Thou Art* (1560-1568), and *Like Will to Like* (1562-1568) lead to *The Alchemist*—not to *Sapho and Phao* or *Loves Metamorphosis*.

There is, however, another form of fifteenth- and sixteenth-century "entertainment" to which Lyly probably owed a considerable debt. In his discussion of Pageant Theatres of the Streets, Glynne Wickham writes:

It is not, however, until the latter half of the sixteenth century that the range of mythological characters in the pageants is seriously widened. Their introduction was not helpful to the vitality of the pageant tradition: for although they obviously increased the spectacular possibilities, their use as speakers was limited to compliment rather than to direct instruction. . . . Nevertheless, the occasional use in England (frequent on the continent) of characters from classical mythology to assist in the delivery of these theatrical homilies on politics, economics and government, provided a precedent for a dramatist who had the ear of the Court to extend their conjoined presence and purpose to regular drama.[2]

Such a dramatist was John Lyly, who had, indeed, the ear of the court. Lyly is sometimes credited with providing a treasure-house of new characters from Classical mythology, but actually nothing new existed in presenting mythological characters on a stage. Lyly's originality lies, instead, in associating the mythological personages with human lovers drawn from the Classical tradition of Roman comedy. In this association he was innovative, and herein lies his greatest legacy to his successors in the romantic comedy.

The basic impulse of Roman comedy is the erotic impulse—boy sees girl, boy wants girl, but boy cannot have girl (at least not immediately).[3] With the exception of *Midas*, all of Lyly's comedies ring changes on this basic Roman formula. In *Alexander and Campaspe*, two men pursue one girl; in *Sapho and Phao*, a variation is introduced whereby two women pursue one man; in *Gallathea*, a more imaginative variation presents a girl (disguised as a boy) pursuing another girl (disguised as a boy). One of the girl-boys finally wins the other—who, by then, is a boy-girl.

Although the erotic impulse is usually powerful in Lyly's comedies, love is sometimes sacrificed to other concerns. Through his use of mythological personages, Lyly invests his plays with a cosmic significance not present in Plautus or Terence. The subplot of *Endimion*, for example, presents Sir Tophas, Lyly's version of the braggart soldier who derives from Plautus's Pyrgopolynices through Nicholas Udall's Ralph Roister Doister. But, unlike Lyly's predecessors, who satirize human folly, he stresses the role of the supernatural and the unattainable in the lives of men.

The following analyses focus on the themes and techniques of Lyly's comedies. Stress falls on his reliance upon Classical models, his independence from tradition, and his unique ironic vision. The order of the plays follows that which is summarized in the Appendix to Peter Saccio's *John Lyly*.[4]

I Alexander and Campaspe (*January 1, 1583/4*)

In Lyly's *Alexander and Campaspe*, Alexander the Great, momentarily forsaking the pursuits of the battlefield and acting against the strenuous objections of his friend and compatriot Hephaestion, hires an artist, Apelles, to paint a portrait of Campaspe, a Theban girl whom Alexander has captured and with whom he has fallen in love. Apelles and Campaspe are eventually attracted to each other but, unwilling to anger Alexander, continue to feign indifference. In order to remain near Campaspe, Apelles damages his painting at the end of each day so that Campaspe will have to sit for him again and again. Alexander finally recognizes the passion shared by the lovers, sacrifices his own claim to Campaspe, consents to a union between the two, and returns to the campgrounds. A subplot involves a number of famous Greek philosophers who discourse with Alexander; and the most cynical of them, Diogenes, provides variety and wit, as does his servant, Manes.[5]

In *Campaspe*, Lyly creates a triangle involving one aristocrat and two commoners. Although this triangle is repeated in Robert Greene's *Friar Bacon and Friar Bungay* (1590?), it is not particularly suited to a love intrigue. Elizabethan comedy, unlike its Roman predecessor, aims not only at sexual fulfillment but also at marriage. But Alexander can no more marry Campaspe than Prince Edward can marry Margaret, the fair maid of Fressingfield. Thus, both *Campaspe* and *Friar Bacon* turn on the theme of magnanimity rather than love; for Alexander and Prince Edward literally give away their loves. Furthermore, neither Alexander nor Prince Edward suffers much from his sacrifice—both have more pressing problems to settle.

Apelles meets Campaspe, Apelles wants Campaspe, but Apelles cannot have Campaspe because Alexander the Great wants her! Since a poor painter can do nothing about such an obstacle as Alexander, he prolongs his own occupation as portrait painter by damaging Campaspe's portrait just before it is completed. The action of the play thus becomes an action of delay—not a satisfying dramatic action. In order to enliven the action, Lyly dips into Pliny and presents Diogenes and the other philosophers, none of whom has much to do with the main love triangle.

Most great drama, be it tragedy or comedy, depends on dramatic irony for effect. That gap in awareness which exists when the audience is in possession of information that is withheld from the participants in the drama is the single most effective element in drama. Sophocles's *Oedipus Rex* would not move the audience nearly so deeply if it did not know the terrible truth that Oediphus is seeking. Shakespeare's *Comedy of Errors* would be unintelligible if the reader did not know that two sets of identical twins are on the loose in Ephesus, a fact hidden from the participants. Nor, for that matter, would Bassanio's choice in the casket scene in *The Merchant of Venice* be exciting if one did not know which casket holds the portrait of Portia. In *Campaspe*, Lyly works less with dramatic irony than he does in subsequent plays. The spectator knows, of course, about Apelles's damaging of Campaspe's portrait, knowledge withheld from Alexander until quite late in the play. Generally speaking, however, in *Campaspe* Lyly sacrifices dramatic irony for more obvious comic devices—puns, quibbles, slapstick, caricature.

J. Dover Wilson calls *Campaspe* the first romantic drama in English, as well as one of the first English dramas with an historical background. Furthermore, Wilson adds, by endowing Campaspe with wit ("A wit apt to conceive and quickest to answer"), Lyly "leads us on the high-road of comedy leading to Congreve."[6] Such criticism may be a shade overenthusiastic, but no more extreme, certainly, than the opposite view expressed by Hereward T. Price: "Lyly does not know what drama is. He shows no conflict between Alexander and Campaspe or Alexander and Apelles or within Alexander himself. Lyly writes some exciting scenes but the play gets bogged down in a morass of disquisition. It is in effect a euphuistic novel."[7]

G. K. Hunter, who includes *Campaspe* in the group of plays unified around debate, claims that Lyly patterns his incidents, shows, and scenes to form illustrations round a central debate-theme: Does true kingliness consist in the power to control others or in the power to command   ourselves? As far as Hunter is concerned, the play belongs to Alexander. The plot focuses attention on Alexander, but not on any single aspect of his life: "We move round the various aspects of his courtesy—his capacity to be magnanimous to all men—gathering new information as we respectfully circle his royalty."[8] In keeping with this view, Hunter transforms Lyly's weakness into a virtue. Lyly's real task in *Campaspe*, according to Hunter, was to find a way to display Alexander's love for Campaspe without seeming to know too much about royal emotions. What Lyly does, in fact, is to present an Alexander who is unaware that love presents a danger to him. As a result, no dramatic intensity is realized in the Alexander-Campaspe situation; but Hunter argues that such was Lyly's intention, for only in this way can he show Alexander as defeated by love and as a conqueror over it. To view the play in this way, however, supports Price's contention that Lyly "shows no conflict."

Peter Saccio argues that Hunter's debate theme does not, in fact, unify *Campaspe*. Instead, Saccio claims that the comedy has no "central dramatic thrust or unity" in plot or character development.[9] The play is unified not through debate, but through allegory, but not the topical variety that equates dramatic characters in *Campaspe* with real Elizabethan ladies and courtiers. It is, rather, an allegory in which the elements of Euphuism, propriety, and decorum yield a universal picture "of the duties of men and of their places among one another."[10] Saccio's description of the variety in *Campaspe* is striking:

There is physical spectacle: the spoils of Thebes and the mythological paintings of Apelles. There is spectacle in the variety of characters; philosophers debate the *ens entium*, page-boys indulge in quips, and a courtesan frolics and sings with her customers. Set speeches on a variety of topics abound: Alexander and Hephestion deliver orations in praise and dispraise of love; Apelles delivers a blazon on Campaspe's beauty; Diogenes harangues a crowd with forceful invective. There are two catechisms: a scholarly one between Alexander and the philosophers, and an erotic one between Apelles and Campaspe. We hear songs and see feats of dancing and acrobatics. The range of verbal and visual display yields entertainment in its most basic sense: the play is a showcase of different kinds of delightful performance.[11]

To describe *Campaspe* is to picture its variety, but Saccio insists that these scenes are woven into a dramatic unity—but not by plot, for *Campaspe* has no plot; not by character development, for there is no sustained depiction of character. What one does have, according to Saccio, are "public, abstract characters, characters whose essence is a position in the structure of the world."[12] It is when men fail to realize their essences that the fictive world of *Campaspe* collapses. The characters are conceived according to a law of decorum: "They are mobilized in incidents selected to present a general idea of propriety, of the duties of men and of their places among one another."[13] It is in propriety, therefore, that Saccio discovers the play's unity. Or, in Saccio's own words, "The individual characters and the particular ideas that appear in *Campaspe* are like nodes or cruces. The anecdotes and their juxtaposition weave lines of relationship among these nodes; they create an elaborately reticulated pattern. Each line of reticulation involves a particular kind of propriety, the kind that governs that particular situation. As a whole the reticulation creates the idea of propriety as a universal, illuminating the total spectacle presented to us."[14]

Saccio's interpretation of *Campaspe*, although remarkably ingenious, is based on assumptions that are not borne out by the text. The most crucial of these are that the chief character is Alexander and that his relationship with Campaspe constitutes the central love story. Alexander, it is true, has the greatest number of lines in the play, but he appears in only five scenes.[15] The bulk of his lines occur at the beginning and at the end; in the crucial third and fourth acts, he appears only once.[16] He serves as a frame, not as the central figure of the play. A frame exists for the sake of the picture, and Alexander exists for the sake of other characters.

The play belongs to Apelles and Campaspe. Their love, not Alexander's, constitutes the central love story. Although Apelles has sixty-four fewer lines than Alexander,[17] he appears in four more scenes,[18] and one feels his presence more. Furthermore, he is present at the emotional center of the comedy. He appears not at all in the first two acts, but in nine of the last fourteen scenes. Finally, Lyly assigns to Apelles the most important speech in the play,[19] as well as the delightful lyric "Cupid and my Campaspe."

If one sees Apelles as the central character and his love the central element, then the structure becomes more readily observable. Saccio insists that "one will not find any kind of plot at all in *Cam-*

paspe."[20] He says also that Elizabethan dramatic criticism, where it discusses comedy, is almost exclusively concerned with the Classical tradition and is useless in explaining Lyly's dramaturgy, for *Campaspe* is not in the Roman tradition. In fact, Saccio says that "except in *Mother Bombie,* Lyly did not write anything like a Roman comedy."[21] It would be truer to say that Lyly seldom wrote anything that was not in the Roman tradition, for where else did Lyly find the central erotic intrigue that motivates most of his comedies? Where else does he find the witty pages and clever servants, the braggart soldier, the crusty father, the youthful lover? As Lyly develops as a dramatist, his debt to Roman comedy increases. In *Campaspe,* Alexander is not overthrown by a clever servant because the play is about royal magnanimity. Alexander does not have to be overcome; he capitulates.

What, then, is the function of Alexander? Hunter indicates the answer when he writes that "the emotions of the 'two loving worms,' Apelles and Campaspe, can only be meaningful if they are recognized by the world of courtly virtue and given status by the royal assent of Alexander; the fulfillment of romantic expectations cannot end the kind of play that Lyly has written."[22] Hunter's view can account for the function of Alexander, but what of Diogenes and the other philosophers? If an explanation is required, Lyly was a practicing playwright, not a critical theorist. His success depended on filling the theater, not on writing highly unified comedies. Saccio admits that the Elizabethans had no notion of the well-made play, but he refuses to admit the delight that can be occasioned by nonce humor. Sidney deplored plays that violated the Classical unities of time, place, and action (as they were understood in the Renaissance); but almost every Elizabethan play violated them. A unified play has no guarantee of success, but a vigorous variety show always attracts its share of customers.

The problem posed by Diogenes is thus crucial to an understanding of Lyly's esthetics. Lyly did not invent the Diogenes episode—it was provided for him in Diogenes Laertius's *Vitae Philosophorum.* Lyly's problem was whether to retain the Diogenes episode or not. But how could he neglect it? Diogenes, the crabbed misogynist, is a playwright's dream—it would be a mighty poor craftsman who could not capitalize on him. His "sharp readiness of tongue and mind, his direct and mordant criticism of society, his seriousness of purpose wrapped in a cloak of mocking raillery, and the wry singularity of his character"[23] insure for him a popularity that needs no further explanation.

Diogenes is important also in that he stands at the opposite extreme to Campaspe. During the Renaissance, Diogenes was noted as an antifeminist, and as such he functions as the polar opposite to the temptations represented by Campaspe. If Alexander is tempted by Campaspe, on the one hand, to forsake his proper duties as ruler, he is tempted, on the other, by the effrontery and apparent honesty of Diogenes. Alexander moves between Campaspe and Diogenes, just as Prince Hal moves between Hotspur and Falstaff: attracted by both, he succumbs to neither.

Campaspe begins with a subsidiary theme. After the exposition, Lyly builds on the theme of the philosopher king. He shows that philosophy is, like most things in his universe, prized according to the position from which it is viewed. Alexander believes that philosophy can come to the aid of good government, but Lyly shows that some philosophers praise the soul at the expense of the body. The jests of Manes, for example, are based on Plato's notion that the body is a prison-house for the soul:

MANES.   I will prove that my body was immortall:
         because it was in prison.
GRAN.   As how?
MANES.   Didde your maisters never teach you that
         the soule is immortall?
GRAN.   Yes.
MANES.   And the body is the prison of the soule.
GRAN.   True.
MANES.   Why then, thus to make my body immortal,
         I put it to prison. (I.ii.30-39)

No lofty philosophic speculation is safe from contamination in Lyly's fictive universe. No words, furthermore, are a satisfactory substitute for reality. Diogenes's servant, Manes, is starving; and Apelles's apprentice, Psyllus, is not much better off since his master feeds him on paintings rather than on food. Both philosopher and painter tend to forget the demands of common humanity, but Alexander does not. In his first encounter with Campaspe, he quickly indicates that her needs will be looked after and that she will want for nothing.[24] The philosophers may be able to teach Alexander something about the nature of abstract thought; but in the art of good government, he must teach them.

Irony is created by the juxtaposition of the first two scenes in Act I. In the first, the tone is serious and businesslike; in the second, light and bantering. In the first, one is led to expect great results from the visit of the philosophers; in the second, one sees what one can really expect. The irony derives also from an awareness that the light tone of the second scene is laid, like a veneer, over the coarser grain of the first scene, over the grim knowledge that some men have empty bellies. It is significant that Act I, Scene ii concludes with a song.[25] Although art cannot replace food, it can express man's hopes and aspirations. The desires of Manes and Psyllus—Granichus appears to be well treated by Plato—find their emotional release in song. The proverbial "wine, women, *and* song" is here translated into its visual equivalent, as wine and women are celebrated *in* song.

One is now prepared to meet the philosophers about whom one has heard so much. First, however, Melippus relates his experiences in gathering them together. He polarizes the group, placing Crisippus at one end and Diogenes at the other; in between, he places Plato, Aristotle, and the rest. Crisippus, so dedicated to study that he neglects his body, neither eating, moving, nor talking, is contrasted to Diogenes, who is only too ready to talk with, or rail at, anyone. Diogenes, however, preserves the outward dignity of philosophy; he will let Alexander come to him, for he will not go to Alexander.

Campaspe is, among other things, a satire against war and philosophy. This attitude is not surprising; for Lyly, although not a Humanist in the strict sense, comes from an illustrious line of professional Humanists, not the least of whom was his grandfather, William Lily, the famous grammarian. Although the courtier admired war, the Humanist sought peace. Alexander, for instance, is a man of war and fit for nothing else but war. Philosophy, as will be seen, falls far too short of reality to serve any useful purpose. Plato's notion of the philosopher-king is fractured and subjected to a realistic analysis which indicates that, sad though it may be, philosophers are not kings, and kings are not philosophers. Indeed, neither can be the other! Although Alexander may be powerful in arms and humane with his captives, he cannot teach the virtue which Diogenes claims to possess. And Diogenes, though he claims to possess virtue, is "crooked [not only] in his shape" but also in his spirit; and he grunts "like a pig under a tub" (I.iii.23).

One finally encounters four of the philosophers—Plato, Aristotle, Cleanthes, Anaxarchus—engaged in lively debate about a suitably lofty theme: whether nature or God is behind creation. Lyly, who is not much interested in philosophical speculation, uses it simply to introduce more pressing matters. Here, for example, the crucial problem is—how is philosophy related to politics? How can these philosophers help Alexander rule more effectively?

At this point, the philosophers are joined by Alexander, Hephaestion, Parmenio, and Clitus. Alexander notes that the philosophers are gathered before him, and Hephaestion's reply clearly establishes the priorities in a militaristic world where philosophy must wait upon the ruler—"They were not Philosophers, if they knew not their dueties" (I.iii.53). This point is later reinforced when Alexander says, "In kinges causes I will not stande to schollers arguments" (I.iii.76). In other words, philosophers and scholars may "instructe the young with rules, confirme the olde with reasons" (I.iii.78); but statecraft remains the prerogative of governors.

The philosophers are tested by Alexander, who asks them a number of riddles. Their replies please Hephaestion, who says, "Would I leaue war, to studie wisdom, were I *Alexander*" (I.iii.101). Alexander, however, is not convinced, as his reply to Hephaestion indicates: "So would I, were I *Hephaestion*" (I.iii.102). The riddles also reinforce the theme of the limitations of philosophy: it is too far removed from reality to be of use to rulers. It may delight the young, like Hephaestion, and serve the old, like Aristotle and Plato; but for the bulk of mankind it lacks utility. Philosophy cannot, for example, release the Theban captives, but Alexander can.

At this moment, when philosophy appears to have been eclipsed, Diogenes, the crabbed philosopher about whom one has heard so much, appears. He is everything one has been led to expect—bold, cantankerous, and magnificent. He is probably the most engaging English comic-stage personality before Falstaff. Diogenes argues for the absolutism of philosophy—kings must wait on philosophers—and criticizes the other philosophers for playing the roles of courtiers. It is tempting to view Diogenes as a spokesman for truth in a world of false flatterers, but Anaxarchus's words— "in contemning him, wee shall better please him" (I.iii.131-132)—place him instead in the camp of Molière's Alceste: he is a man who rails for the sake of railing.

Whatever his deficiencies as a philosopher, Diogenes has few equals in a quarrel. In Act I, Scene iii, Lyly brought Diogenes into conflict with his peers. In Act II, Scene i, he brings him into conflict with Psyllus, Manes, and Granichus, the clever pages; and again Diogenes's wit is superior. Much of the humor in this scene is derived from puns on Latin phrases, and "footnote humor" is about all that remains for the modern reader. Even the Latin phrases themselves no longer carry the force that once could provoke laughter.

The following scene (II.ii) is divided into two parts, the first dealing with love; the second, with Diogenes. Alexander declares his love for Campaspe, thus evoking a long anti-romantic, didactic speech from Hephaestion. From the point of view of this professional soldier, love is a feminine, debilitating emotion in all men, but worst of all in a ruler. Besides, Hephaestion adds, women are not to be trusted; fair exteriors hide devious minds. The discussion between Alexander and Hephaestion leads finally to an awareness of the power of love. When Alexander says that he loves Campaspe, "a thing farre vnfit for a Macedonian, for a king, for *Alexander*" (II.ii.20-21), he indicates his helplessness in the grip of love. Hephaestion tries to bring reason to bear, hoping to dissuade Alexander in his pursuit of Campaspe. But, as Alexander points out, reason is not to the point. Yet, as the debate continues, Alexander traps himself in a contradiction. When asked by Hephaestion what he will do if Campaspe rejects him, Alexander replies that it would be unreasonable of her to do so. But if reason is not to the point, then there is no reason why Campaspe should be reasonable. When Hephaestion points out this flaw in Alexander's argument, Haphaestion is silenced by a show of force: Alexander orders him to be silent!

The second part of the scene presents Alexander confronted by Diogenes. Here the limitations of Alexander's power continue to emerge. In the first part of the scene, Alexander's intellect has been successfully challenged by Hephaestion; in this second part, Alexander's system of values is challenged by the cynic—Diogenes. Everything that Alexander considers important, Diogenes holds in contempt:

ALEX.   What doest thou want?
DIOG.   Nothing that you haue.
ALEX.   I haue the world at commaund.
DIOG.   And I in contempt. (II.ii.140-144)

Then, with admirable succinctness, Lyly expresses dramatically the ultimate limitation imposed on humanity, royal or otherwise:

ALEX.   Thou shalt liue no longer than I will.
DIOG.   But I will die whether you will or no. (II.ii.145-146)

Alexander may be powerful, but over the forces of life he has no control. He may destroy, but he cannot create. His claim that he is a God of the Earth (II.ii.129) becomes an empty boast in the light of Diogenes's contempt for the world.

In Act II, Scene ii, Alexander is defeated both by Hephaestion's inescapable logic and by Diogenes's contempt. He can silence Hephaestion only by royal command; Diogenes, he cannot silence at all. In short, Alexander, the man of war, is bested by the man of reason and by the spokesman for misanthropy. Alexander can command neither love nor wisdom. Thus the figure of Diogenes is brought into closer union with the theme of love versus reason which dominates the last three acts of the comedy.

In the third act, the love-game comedy begins in earnest when Apelles pleads helplessness in the face of Campaspe's great beauty. Actually, the love triangle has its origin in Roman comedy, where young lovers are often kept apart by an interfering older, wealthier suitor. There is in *Campaspe*, of course, some departure from the Roman formula. At first Apelles does not want Campaspe, nor she him. In fact, both are anti-Petrarchan lovers, embryo Benedicts and Beatrices. Appelles is only too conscious of Campaspe's feminine wiles, and she is terribly businesslike in her dealings with him. But they do fall in love. An obstacle, however, must be overcome, an obstacle posed by Alexander, who is in the position of the older, wealthier, not to mention more powerful, suitor of Roman comedy. Lyly introduces an additional departure, however, in that Alexander cannot be overthrown since he represents royal authority. There-fore, the play has no manipulator, no witty parasite or servant who, in league with the young lovers, eliminates the obstacle represented by the older suitor. In *Campaspe*, Alexander must eliminate himself, thus removing the play from the genre of intrigue com-edies.

After a brief interruption in the form of a comic scene involving the servants, the love game resumes with a lesson in mythology (stories about unnatural love), before, during, and after which Apel-les assumes the role of a prostrate lover and tries to entice Cam-paspe with talk of love. She is too clever for him, however, and puns her way free.

In the first part of Act III, Scene iv (1-27), Clitus and Parmenio, two professional soldiers, serve as commentators about Alexander's emotional problems and about his function as ruler. Lyly chooses this indirect method to illustrate Alexander's frustrations in love because it permits him to portray the mighty ruler as a mooning lover but, at the same time, to introduce fresh attitudes about the subject of love. Neither Clitus nor Parmenio believes that Alexander is really in love, for each equates love with weakness and speaks of the "weak conceites of loue" (III.iv.18).

In the second part of the scene, which resumes the discussion between Alexander and Hephaestion which was earlier cut short (in II.ii), Alexander copes with Hephaestion's jibes more reasonably:

HEP.   You loue, and therefore think any thing.
ALEX.   But not so far in loue with *Campaspe*, as with Bucephalus, if occa-
         sion serue either of cõflicte or of conquest. (III.iv.31-32)

But Alexander's boast lacks probity, and Hephaestion is quick to point out that an occasion is not wanting, since the Persians, Scithians, and Egyptians are all to be conquered. Alexander, who refuses to face Hephaestion's objections, takes refuge instead in his own self-created image which will not permit him to admit that he is a captive of love: "Doubt not but *Alexander* can, when he wil, throw affections as farre from him as he can cowardise" (III.iv.43-44).

After a comic interlude which presents Diogenes and Alexander both refusing to loan money to Crysus, the fourth part of Act III,

Scene iv (58-127), develops further the theme of Alexander's
limitations. As he is unfit to play the part of a philosopher, so is he
unfit to play the part of a painter. His simplistic view of reality leads
him to believe that a painter need use only four colors when he
momentarily dons the painter's frock. But, alas! Alexander paints
like a king, not like a painter.

Lyly turns now to Apelles to present the painter in love, and he
permits traditional form to operate again as Apelles laments his
situation. After all, how could Campaspe select him in preference to
the "monarch of the earth"? To gain time, Apelles takes a hint from
Homer's Penelope and plans to damage Campaspe's portrait so that
she will return for additional sittings. The scene concludes with the
famous song which, in the stage directions, is assigned to Apelles
and suggests his collapse in the face of love:

> *Cupid* and my *Campaspe* playd
> At Cardes for kisses, *Cupid* payd;
> He stakes his Quiuer, Bow, & Arrows,
> His Mothers doues, & teeme of sparows;
> Looses them too; then, downe he throwes
> The corrall of his lippe, the rose
> Growing on's cheek (but none knows how),
> With these, the cristall of his Brow,
> And then the dimple of his chinne:
> All these did my *Campaspe* winne.
> At last, hee set her both his eyes;
> Shee won, and *Cupid* blind did rise.
>   O Loue! has shee done this to Thee?
>   What shall (Alas!) become of mee? (III.v.62-75)

To appreciate the advance in sophistication of language represented by *Campaspe* over preceding English comedy, one need only
contrast Lyly's admirable lyric with a song from, say, *Ralph Roister
Doister:*

> Whoso to marry a minion wife
>   Hath had good chance and hap,
> Must love her and cherish her all his life,
>   And dandle her in his lap.
> If she will fare well, if she will go gay,

> A good husband ever still,
> Whatever she lust to do, or to say,
> Must let her have her own will: (I.iv.113-20)[26]

The fourth act returns to Diogenes, who has attracted an audience by his promise to fly. Instead of flying, however, he indulges himself in flyting, as he castigates the citizens for unbecoming conduct. When faced with the fact of his own immorality—he has been seen leaving a brothel—he threatens to spread lies about the citizens of Athens. If they call him a liar for failing to fly, he will say the Athenians are mischievous.

Earlier (III.v), Apelles lamented his discomfort caused by unrequited love. Now (IV.ii) Campaspe laments her choice of a lover, thus reinforcing the theme of irrationality in love. Sought by a prince, Campaspe chooses a painter! She rationalizes her choice by complaining that her base birth must have left her with a base mind. But, given the fact of her love for Apelles, she sets about to discover his true feelings about her. The love game resumes as the remainder of the scene is devoted to a battle of wits between the young lovers. The game encourages mutual suspicion, however, and the scene concludes with the lovers still at odds. The following scene (IV.iii) reminds one of Alexander's military functions, for his soldiers complain that he has neglected his campaigns for the soft couches of love. Alexander is compared with his father, Philip, and found wanting.

By Act IV, Scene iv, the love game is partly over as Campaspe and Apelles declare their love for each other, but they fail to take Alexander into their confidence. One obstacle has been removed (the internal obstacle posed by themselves), but one still remains (the obstacle represented by Alexander). So formidable is the second obstacle that the lovers despair of ever achieving happiness together. Campaspe's soliloquy, which assumes the form of a second lament, occupies the remainder of Act IV, Scene iv. When Campaspe evaluates her position at this point in the proceedings, romance dissolves in the face of reality. She fears that, in revealing her love to Apelles, she has undone herself. But, what alternative had she? Apelles's love stems from his heart; Alexander's, from his mouth. Besides, Alexander is a king; and "in kinges there can be no loue, but to Queenes; for as neere must they meete in maiestie, as they doe in affection" (IV.iv.30-31).

The following scene (IV.v) presents a parallel action as Apelles acknowledges the danger he runs in becoming a rival to Alexander. The fourth act thus ends on a note of *angst*. The question, never asked but always present, is: what will Alexander do when he finds out that Campaspe loves Apelles? The love of Campaspe and Apelles works itself out against a backdrop of resentment and threat. In the fifth act, Lyly relaxes one's emotions for a moment as he brings back Diogenes, who plays a scene with a citizen, Sylvius, and his three sons. The scene (V.i), a burlesque of the convention whereby a father brings his children to a famous teacher for instruction, has practically no relevance; it is actually an interlude in which dancing, tumbling, and singing, not debate or rhetoric, provide the entertainment.

Apelles's second lament (V.ii), like Campaspe's first lament (IV.ii), stresses the irrationality of love: "I must endure intollerable passions, for vnknowne pleasures. Dispute not the cause, wretch, but yeeld to it: for better it is to melt with desire, than wrastle with loue" (10-12). Like Pygmalion, Apelles has fallen in love with his own creation: "O *Campaspe*, I haue painted thee in my heart: painted? nay, contrarye to myne arte, imprinted, and that in such deepe Characters, that nothing can rase it out, vnlesse it rubbe my heart out" (14-17).

In the following scene (V.iii), Lyly again switches from love to philosophy, from Apelles to Diogenes. This scene reinforces a point introduced casually in Act IV, Scene i (55). There, Selinus has accused Diogenes of frequenting brothels; now, Lais accuses Diogenes of soliciting her favors. "The time was," she says, "thou wouldest haue hadde my company, had it not beene, as thou saidst, too deare" (28-9). Since lack of money is the apparent source of Diogenes's virtue, his supposed moral superiority is the result of his inability to be immoral. So much for philosophy!

Perhaps the real philosophers in the play are Milectus and Phrygius, who, juxtaposed as they are to the militaristic Parmenio and Clitus, remind one that wars maim and kill men. Under the cover of a bawdy joke, Phrygius effectively points the moral: "Downe with armes, and up with legges, this is a world for the nonce" (V.iii.2-3). Although their social credentials are not of the best sort, these disenchanted soldiers offer refreshing Falstaffian views about the occupation held in such high esteem by Alexander.

Somewhere between Act IV, Scene iii, and Act V, Scene iv, Alexander's enthusiasm for Campaspe has begun to wane. Becoming suspicious about Apelles's affection for Campaspe, Alexander arranges for a little play to be staged. Apelles will be told that his studio is on fire, whereupon he will rush inside and save the work most dear to him. And the work? Why, Campaspe's portrait, of course. As his play is being staged, Alexander questions Hephaestion about love and receives the following description: love, says Hephaestion, is "a word by superstition thought a god, by vse turned to an humour, by selfwil made a flattering madnesse" (V.iv.35-36). This description, then, provides one of the extremes between which Alexander moves in this play. The other can be found in the love between Apelles and Campaspe. Alexander is neither so harsh as Hephaestion ("you are to hard harted to think so of loue," he tells Hephaestion [V.iv.37]), nor so soft as Apelles.

The final view of Diogenes is one in which Alexander puts a number of questions to him (a repetition of I.iii.83ff), the last of which concerns love. Like Hephaestion, Diogenes assumes an extreme position; and Alexander again strikes a moderate pose as he admonishes Diogenes: "Thou wert neuer born of woman, that thou thinkest so hardly of womē" (V.iv.68-69). Nevertheless, Alexander announces his intention to study philosophy with Diogenes, an announcement which puts the lid on the theme of royal limitation introduced in Act II, Scene ii, when Hephaestion told Alexander that he was powerless to control love. Now Lyly shows that Alexander is deficient in knowledge as well as in power. The audience knows that Diogenes is deformed, both in body and spirit, and that his "virtue" is a façade. Alexander, however, sees only a stubbornness which he mistakes for individualism and integrity.

A true child of his own stubbornness, Diogenes puts the quietus on any plans Alexander might have of becoming a philosopher when he announces that he will not associate with a courtier. From Diogenes's point of view, then, one may be either a philosopher *or* a courtier, but not both. It is an interesting point, one which Hunter could have used in support of his hypothesis that by Lyly's time the Humanist ceased to serve any real purpose in court.[27] Or, in other words, by Lyly's time the trained philosopher was no longer prized by kings.

The play ends, as it began, with two characters alone on stage. Alexander congratulates himself for his ability to resist love, and Hephaestion gives his enthusiastic approval. Alexander has apparently learned self-control. Hunter appears to be on safe ground in contending that the play consists of various scenes illustrating the nature of true kingliness; that is, does kingliness consist in the power to control others or in the power to control oneself?[28] Alexander seems to be in control of himself once again. He seems to have regained the victor's laurel which he wore at the start of the action. Yet, in Lyly's plays, appearances can never be trusted. Does not Alexander's very last sentence suggest that his victory over love is at best illusory:

> And good *Hephestion,* when al the world is woone,
> and euery countrey is thine and mine, either find
> me out an other to subdue, or of my word I wil
> fall in loue. (V.iv 153-155)

Saccio mentions that the fifth act of *Campaspe* is complicated;[29] it is more complicated than he imagines. Lyly is never satisfied with the obvious—he delights in playing tricks; and he catches his audience up short at the end of *Campaspe.* If the audience has believed that Alexander's "conversion" is real, it must make a sudden adjustment; for Alexander's victory over himself is about as real as Diogenes's victory over Lais and the other ladies of easy virtue. Both Alexander and Diogenes are frauds—attractive frauds, perhaps, but frauds nevertheless. Their "victories" result from impotence, not from the power of rule or the force of will. Diogenes does not have enough money to buy Lais's favors; Alexander does not have enough power to sway Campaspe's affections. Neither, in short, can have what he wants, so each settles for something else: Diogenes for "philosophizing"; Alexander for conquering.

The characters least affected by self-deception are, of course, Campaspe and Apelles. The "two loving wormes" are thus rewarded for their ingenuity and persistence. They alone of the major characters need not dip into the salve of self-righteousness to sooth their injured vanities. They get what they want; but, although their love constitutes the central love interest in the play, Lyly's final interest is in Alexander, not in the lovers. For this reason, he removes

Campaspe and Apelles from the stage at the end, permitting only Alexander and Hephaestion to remain. In this sense, at least, the play is Alexander's, but Alexander's victory is not what the play is all about.

Seen in this light, *Campaspe* is hardly the allegory that many critics would make it.[30] An Alexander who finds comfort in self-deception, a king whose power is pitifully limited, is an unlikely parallel to Queen Elizabeth. There are, furthermore, sentiments expressed that are impossible to explain by any allegorical framework. For example, Parmenio complains that kings "have long eares and stretched armes, in whose heades suspition is a proofe, and to be accused is to be condemned" (III.iv.6-8). This statement is hardly the kind of tribute that would ingratiate Lyly to Elizabeth. Even greater strain is placed upon the allegorical hypothesis in *Sapho and Phao*, where the queen Sapho is described at one point as tossing and turning in a hot bed of chastity itching for her beloved Phao (III.iii)—another unlikely parallel to England's virgin queen. The only way the allegorical argument can be sustained is by nelecting passages which offer contradictory testimony. The plays are full of speeches which are at best unflattering to royalty and at worst insulting.[31]

II   Sapho and Phao *(March 3, 1583/4)*

Sapho and Phao marks an advance over *Campaspe* in Lyly's dramatic development. The structure is tighter, the themes clearer, and the characterization more sharply defined. The quest for variety, always a hallmark of Lyly, is more restrained in *Sapho and Phao* than in its predecessor, with perhaps a corresponding loss of vitality.

In order to humble the proud queen Sapho, Venus takes an ordinary ferryman, Phao, and makes him irresistibly handsome. Although he feels the cravings of desire, he treats all women with an exquisite scorn until he meets Sapho, at which moment a mutual passion is enkindled. Ironically, Venus falls victim to her own devices as she too falls in love with Phao. Helplessly in love, she tries to get Cupid to undo her own handiwork and to separate Sapho and Phao. Cupid does manage to disengage Sapho's affections, but he then betrays his mother by instilling in Phao a loathing for her. Unable to comprehend his rejection by Sapho, Phao returns to his native land as Cupid takes up his residence with Sapho.

In *Sapho and Phao*, irony of situation plays a key role. Lyly does not, however, exploit dramatic irony as he eventually does in *Gallathea*. Although most of the participants do not share with the audience the knowledge that Venus is the force behind Phao's transformation, little information of importance is withheld from the participants.

Sapho is the first of Lyly's comedies that does not end with wedding bells or marriage feasts—it is not the last. In this respect, *Sapho* is more characteristic of Lyly's mature style than is *Campaspe*. Lyly's way is not the way of marriage feasts and wedding bells. It is, rather, the way of melancholy bitterness, of mingled grief and joy; a vision concocted of many simples, it is complex in the extreme. This frustration of the erotic impulse may have led Lyly to define *Endimion* as "Neither Comedie, nor Tragedie"[32]—a definition equally applicable to *Sapho* and *The Woman in the Moon*.

Sapho is also the first of Lyly's comedies to employ a practicer, a character who willfully deceives others. In fact, Venus is both the practicer and the external obstacle in the play. In kindling a mutual passion between Sapho and Phao, she is a practicer; in trying to win Phao for herself, she represents the external obstacle. But, in falling into her own trap, Venus becomes the victim as well. She thus fulfills three separate functions, and she is Lyly's most sophisticated characterization to date. The spectacle of the goddess of love hoist on her own petard is indeed a richly comic one.

J. Dover Wilson calls Lyly the "father of English comedy" because he realized that the true pivot of comedy is the woman, and he capitalized upon the realization. The first of his exquisite female characters is Sapho, "the haughty but amorous queen."[33] Campaspe, perhaps because of her somewhat helpless and docile position in *Alexander and Campaspe*, was never able to give free expression to the wit and subtlety that characterizes Sapho, a queen, who dominates, so far as purely human domination is possible, the situation.

The situation in *Sapho and Phao* is similar to that in *Alexander and Campaspe* in that a love triangle motivates the action, but the similarity gives way to originality of conception in *Sapho* as Lyly reverses the triangle. In *Campaspe*, as T. W. Baldwin points out, two men are rivals for one woman; in *Sapho*, two women for one man.[34] Sapho and Venus replace Alexander and Apelles, but the solution is reversed as well. In *Campaspe*, one of the rivals carries off the prize; in *Sapho*, no one wins. Jonas Barish regards the ending as an example of Lyly's inability to resolve character conflicts. Barish argues that Lyly's imagination leads him "to pit character against character and motive against motive with great skill, but it leaves him helpless to cope with the very different requirements of denouement."[35] Lyly is able to disjoin character and analyze feeling to create dramatic effect but he can do little to fuse or rejoin them.

Others would argue that it is not Lyly's analytic imagination that accounts for what Barish considered poor endings, but it is his selection of characters. Sapho, for example, falls in love with a commoner; and queens do not marry ferrymen. Although democracy was making inroads in the sixteenth century, it had not progressed this far. By the same token, Alexander cannot marry Campaspe, Cynthia cannot marry Endimion, and Gunophilus cannot marry Pandora. In each of these instances, Lyly creates a social or metaphysical impasse which makes impossible the usual comic ending. But he does so with such regularity that it is undoubtedly intentional and should not be viewed as a failure. After all, Lyly frequently emphasizes in his prefaces that he is not writing traditional comedy or tragedy.

The two prologues to *Sapho* suggest that Lyly was consciously departing from accepted comic technique. In the "Prologue at the Blackfriars," he appears to be trying to educate his audience in the ways of sophisticated comedy: "Our intēt was at this time to moue inward delight, not outward lightness, and to breede (if it might bee) soft smiling, not loude laughing." In the "Prologue at the Court," Lyly further develops his critical theory: "We present no conceites nor warres, but deceites and loues, wherein the trueth may excuse the plainenesse: the necessitie, the length: the poetrie, the bitternesse." It is impossible to determine precisely what Lyly intends, but he appears to be saying that *Sapho* is a different kind of courtly comedy. First, it differs in subject matter; love, not war, is its theme. Second, it differs in form; plain not conceited. The disparity in subject matter seems clear. *Sapho* is concerned with the amours of a queen; *Campaspe* is concerned, at least in good measure, with the career of a famous martial conqueror.

The difference in form, however, is far from clear. *Sapho* is no less "conceited" than *Campaspe;* in fact, the two plays are remarkably similar. Each play is approximately 1450 lines in length, and each play contains five acts subdivided into nineteen scenes. Each play has a multiple plot structure which turns on a love triangle, and the only major difference lies in the constitution of the triangle and in the denouement. In one respect, however, *Sapho* is less complicated than *Campaspe:* the latter requires twenty-eight speaking parts, but the former requires only seventeen. But this is hardly a distinction that would characterize *Sapho* as a "plain" comedy.

In fact, when one takes into account the presence in *Sapho* of the gods and goddesses, the play becomes more complicated than *Campaspe*. Metaphysical implications are present in *Sapho* that are not found in the earlier play, and they suggest that *Sapho* is certainly not "plain." For the first time, Lyly uses mythological personages; and in his next five plays mythology mingles with or entirely replaces the human element, for good or for ill.

Why Lyly apologizes for the length of *Sapho* is uncertain. In fact, it is uncertain whether he believes it to be too long or too short. By comparison with English comedy written in the 1590's, *Sapho* is short (most Elizabethan plays written for the public stage run to about 2500 lines); but it is about average length for Lyly. Five of his plays (give or take a couple of hundred lines) are about 1500 lines, two about 2000, and one about 1150 lines. Plays written for the private playhouses tended, on the whole, to be shorter than those written for the public stage. There is nothing unusual, then, in the length of *Sapho;* and no apparent reason as to why Lyly was concerned about it exists.

The third point advanced in the "Prologue at the Court," "the bitternesse," is more readily understandable. *Sapho* obviously does not end in typical comic fashion. There are neither wedding bells nor a marriage feast; and Phao, alone and dejected, returns to a life which will no longer yield contentment.

Sapho begins with a statement of one of the major themes—country versus courtly life. Phao's own words best describe his situation: "free," "content," "quiet," "satisfied," "gentle," "sweet," "calm," "delicate." Although Phao is an Arcadian of sorts, he is also a Stoic: "Thy thoughts are no higher thē thy fortunes, nor thy desires greater than thy calling" (2-4). His thatched cottage and his pastoral occupation yield a sweet contentment that is seldom found under a golden roof, but his Utopia is not quite perfect. "The winde," he complains, "is thy greatest enemy, whose might is withstoode with pollicy" (14-15).

Venus, the goddess of love, creates quite a different impression at her initial appearance. Whereas Phao spoke of contentment, sweetness, and calmness, Venus speaks of unseemliness, unwholesomeness, crabbedness, and crookedness. The love goddess thus signifies the bitterness to which love will lead in *Sapho*. Phao, who knows nothing about love, is contented; Venus, who knows everything about love, is discontented. Unhappy with her status as Vulcan's consort, Venus finds an outlet for her discontent in Sapho, a woman reputedly immune to Love's allurements.

The second scene parallels the first, as Lyly substitutes Trachinus, a courtier, and Pandion, a scholar, for Phao and Venus. Convinced of the superiority of experience over formal learning, Trachinus tries to convert Pandion into a courtier. Pandion, however, is a professed truth-seeker and finds distasteful the idea of dissembling, one of the courtier's chief stratagems. The university man is appalled at the insincerity he discovers at court, an insincerity which underlies the courtier's existence. Lyly makes a sharp distinction between the courtier and the scholar (no Hamlets here!), just as he did throughout *Euphues* and its sequel. Like Phao, Pandion has achieved a measure of serenity which has been denied Trachinus. Like Venus, Trachinus is unable—or unwilling—to recognize the nature of tranquillity, and he tries to distort it into his own image.

Lyly has established the premises on which the action turns in *Sapho*: country life is serene; life in the study, fruitful; courtly life, frivolous and insincere. But in Act I, Scene iii, Lyly introduces new characters with fresh points of view to present yet another perspective of the court-versus-study controversy, this time from the underlings. In the eyes of Cryticus, page to Trachinus, and Molus, page to Pandion, both court and study are equally frivolous. Molus points out that scholars tend to get lost when they step outside the halls of academe, and Cryticus vividly describes the activity of a courtier:

We pages are Politians: for looke what we heare our maisters talke of, we determine of: where we suspect, we vndermine: and where we mislike for some perticular grudge, there we pick quarrels for a generall griefe. Nothing amonge vs but in steede of good morow, what newes? wee fal from cogging at dice, to cogge with states: & so forward are meane mē in those matters, that they wold be cocks to tread down others, before they be chickēs to rise themselues. Youthes are very forwarde to stroke their chins, though they haue no beardes, and to lie as lowd as hee that hath liued longest. (24-33)

The theme that Lyly is apparently developing, that of praise of the study at expense of the court, gives way now to a more comprehensive theme, that of *vanitas vanitatum.*

Insincerity at court continues to be the theme in Act I, Scene iv, in which Sapho's ladies-in-waiting discourse on love. These maidens—Mileta, Lamia, Favilla, Ismena, Canope, and Eugenua—reveal their contempt for men and their wooing customs. Mileta strikes a heavy materialistic note in a speech in the "diamonds-are-a-girl's-best-friend" tradition: "Giue me their giftes, not their vertues; a graine of their golde weigheth downe a pound of their witt; a dram of 'giue me,' is heauier than an ounce of 'heare me' " (24-26). In terms of plot, the opening lines of Act I, Scene iv, reveal that Venus has already transformed Phao into an irresistibly attractive man, as his former tranquillity is replaced by disdainful looks and imperious words. This character change reinforces the attitude taken toward love in Act I, Scene i, and prepares for the cynical discussion of love which occurs later in Act I, Scene iv. In *Sapho*, love is not a transcendental experience; it is a journey into disillusionment.

As the second act begins, Venus's curse is operating. Phao is endowed with exceptional beauty, but he is unable to love. He has exchanged his oar for a mirror and is distraught: "O Venus! In thinking thou hast blest me, thou hast curst me, adding to a poore estate, a proud heart; and to a disdained man, a disdaining minde" (3-5). In this disenchanted mood Phao encounters Sybilla, whose career somewhat parallels his own: she, too, has experienced the divine touch. In return for her love, Apollo has granted her long life; but, like Sapho's handmaidens, she dissembled with the god and was cursed with old age. Her advice to Phao reinforces what the reader has already discovered about courtly life. Sybilla is an unmitigated cynic, and for her no course of action can yield a positive result.

Men can remain honest and perish through lack of love and friends, or they can dissemble and perish through lack of sincerity. This either-or formula constitutes an inverted tragic situation and lends a note of bitterness to the play.

The Court claims a momentary victory in Act II, Scene ii, when Sapho engages Phao as her page and when Pandion accepts Trachinus's invitation to be his guest. Both Arcadian and Scholar surrender to the glitter of courtly enticements. The following scene (II.iii) illustrates the nature of the attraction which has captivated Phao and Pandion. The scene is divided into two parts, the first of which (1-32) presents Pandion's servant, Molus, who has been converted to courtly ways. His peculiar specialty is evident from his opening words: "What newes Cryticus?" Molus is a newsmonger, one whose "humour" it is to be "in the know." The remainder of Act II, Scene iii (33ff.), is devoted to an exercise in logic—or illogic. As is so often characteristic of Lyly's servants, the humor turns on words integral to the study of formal logic.

Act II, Scene iv, is also divided into two parts, the first of which (1-36) is devoted to Phao's lament over his newly inspired passion for Sapho (the lament sounds much like those of Philautus in the two narratives).[36] Like Endimion, who literally desires the moon, Phao aspires far above his station in life: "Phao! vnhappy, canst thou not be content to beholde the sunne, but thou muste couet to build thy nest in the Sunne?" (3-4).

Taking his cue from Philautus in *Euphues* and *Euphues and His England*, Phao assumes the role of the romantic lover who is driven close to death by love's agonies. "Die Phao, Phao die" (8), he cries, as he realizes that Sapho's beauty and his own affection for her are beyond his control. Love is divine, he comes to believe, "no more to bee suppressed than comprehended" (17). But he will observe the laws of love and keep his passion secret while he plans his conquest of Sapho. His first step will be to pay a second visit to Sybilla, "whose olde yeares haue not beene idle in these young attemptes, & whose sound aduice may mitigate (though the heavẽs cannot remoue) my miseries" (33-36).

The second part of Act II, Scene iv (37ff.), witnesses a second meeting between Phao and Sybilla (cf. II.i). During this one-sided encounter, Sybilla does all of the talking. Her advice derives from Euphues's exhortations and from Psellus's maxims to Philautus.[37]

She argues that love is an art and that fancy must be ruled by wisdom. Although cynical about women, Sybilla is quite different from Sapho's ladies-in-waiting; for Sybilla portrays them as essentially foolish creatures, too weak and flimsy to withstand the attention of men. According to Sybilla, if a man desires to succeed in love, he need only observe the rules of love, which are rooted in pretense and trickery (cf. especially lines 87-118).

Sybilla's advice creates tension between romantic love and biological love. From her point of view, the irresistible charms of a woman can be secured only at the expense of personal integrity. The frivolous nature of woman militates against a relationship based on mutual trust and understanding. Cunning and cajolery, not reason or respect, are the weapons that overthrow women. But, in the final analysis, women are overthrown because they want to be: "I tell the a straung thing, womenne striue, because they would be ouercome: force they call it, but such a welcome force they account it, that continually they study to be enforced" (92-95).

The following scene (III.i) modifies Sybilla's love theories by presenting a woman helplessly caught in the grip of an irresistible passion. The scene is rife with sexual innuendo when Ismena, Mileta and Pandion wittily discuss the cause of Sapho's sudden illness. No one, however, dares to say outright what he suspects; for Sapho is, after all, a queen and demands respect even when she does not deserve it. When the ladies are called away to attend on Sapho after she "faints," Pandion and Trachinus discuss courtly amours. Nowhere is the falsity and artificiality better criticized than in Pandion's remark, "Why, in courtes there is nothing more common. And as to be bald among the Micanyans it was accounted no shame, because they were all balde: so to be in loue among courtiers it is no discredit: for that they are al in loue" (33-36).

Act III, Scene ii, is devoted to the appetites; the first part, to hunger (1-34); the second, to sex (35-94). Molus and Cryticus jest about Lenten menus in the university and at court before Calypho arrives. With his appearance, the emphasis shifts from the belly to the nether regions. Puns on horns (in the form of parentheses) abound as Vulcan is ridiculed as a cuckold and as Cryticus reveals his secret sexual desires. The scene concludes with a song, as did Act II, Scene iii, when these three characters were last on stage together. The son is blatantly crude and provides a striking contrast with Phao's love for Sapho, not to mention Sybilla's insistence upon the rules of the game. In this song Bacchus reigns; and panders, pimps, and whores rule the day:

> See, see, the Battaile now growes hot,
> Here legs flye, here goes Heads to th' Pot,
> Here Whores and Knaues tosse broken glasses,
> Here all the Souldiers looke like Asses. (81-84)

Act III, Scene iii, picks up the action where it left off in Act III, Scene i, as Sapho, still languishing with love for Phao, is consoled by her ladies-in-waiting. When Eugenua mentions that Phao is skilled in simples, or medicinal herbs, Sapho jumps at the suggestion and sends for him, even though she knows that their respective stations in life prohibit any kind of lasting relationship. Such is the power of love! Momentarily pacified, Sapho falls asleep, whereupon the ladies discuss her strange affliction. Mileta strikes at the heart of romantic love conventions when she, like Shakespeare's Rosalind in *As You Like It*, observes that she did "neuer heare of a woman that died of a conceite" (57-58).

Much of the scene is taken up with Sapho's lament (a repetition of II.iv.1-36) wherein she adumbrates the honor she has always paid to Venus, the danger of giving in to love, the difficulty of not giving in to love, and the impossibility of the situation since Phao is only a ferryman. Sapho may sacrifice her intelligence to love, but not her honor. But when Sapho hears that Phao has arrived *without* his simples, she wants to see him anyway. So much for honor!

Act III, Scene iv, is divided into three parts: the first (1-36) reveals a Phao more than able to defend himself in a courtly battle of wits with Mileta; the second (37-85) is devoted to a guarded exchange of endearments between Sapho and Phao; the third (86-100) registers Venus's reaction upon seeing her handiwork face to face: "O faire Phao, O sweete Phao" (88). Like Pygmalion, Venus has fallen in love with her own creation. The scene finally concludes with a battle of wits between Venus and Phao, with the latter clearly triumphant.

The scene between Sapho and Phao in part two illustrates Robert Y. Turner's contention that Lyly creates circumstances which make it impossible for his lovers to speak their minds. They are forced to

speak enigmatically, partly out of fear and partly out of sensitivity
to the delicate nature of love. "This tension between unfavorable
circumstances and desire creates dialogue in which each assertion is
tentative and each response quivering," says Turner, thus creating a
sense of what it is like to be in love.[38]

Under the protection of a pun (*you—yew*), Sapho and Phao exchange vows of love. Yet the protection is only a pretense, for earlier
they both betrayed an awareness of the impossibility of their situation. Although Phao's complaint that only "Heart's ease" can cure
her, but that it grows too high off the ground (symbolic of her high
station), is countered by Sapho's rejoinder that it, in fact, grows
very low (symbolic of his low station), the obstacle is immovable.

The third act has repeated, with variation, many of the themes
introduced in the first two acts. The agony of love now afflicts
Sapho, just as it afflicted Phao in the second act. Here the palinode
to romantic love comes, not from Sybilla as it did in the second act,
but from Calypho, Cryticus, and Molus. In the second act, Phao attracted a queen; in the third act, he attracts a goddess.

The fourth act consists of four short scenes that analyze the
effects wrought by love. In Act IV, Scene i, Sapho vainly questions
Venus and Cupid regarding their motives in persecuting her. She
finds herself in a dilemma, as indicated by her reply to Venus's
assurance that Phao will yield to her: "If hee yeelde, then shal I
shame to embrace one so meane; if not, die, because I cannot embrace one so meane. Thus do I finde no meane" (15-17). Honor and
love continue to wage their war within the breast of Sapho. In Act
IV, Scene ii, Venus adds her lament to that of Phao (II.iv. 1-36) and
Sapho (III.iii.83-113). Venus has been responsible for Sapho's
loveliness and Phao's fairness; now they love each other, and Venus
suffers from unrequited love. The unnaturalness of romantic love is
illustrated when Venus asks her own son how she can best achieve
sexual satisfaction and is also implicit in Venus's admission that she
is really too old for love (39).

Act IV, Scene iii, is filled with dreams which serve as symbolic
equivalents for Sapho's situation. The first dream is a clear statement of frustrated sexuality, for Sapho imagines she sees a
stockdove unsuccessfully attempting to build his nest in a tall cedar
tree (1-21). The bird's nest is, itself, overtly sexual; the stockdove is,
of course, Phao, who tries to build his nest high up in the cedar tree,

which is, of course, Sapho (in II.iv.4, Phao said that he was trying to build his nest in the sun). Naturally, Sapho hopes that the cedar will bend, as it does in her dream, so that Phao will be able to nest in it.

The other five dreams (IV.iii) are not so clear, which is probably why they are explained, or interpreted, in the text. Mileta's dream is concerned ostensibly with fire, water, and blood; for she pictures herself with her hair aflame, her friend Ismene as attempting to quench the flames, but her friend's efforts to brush away the sparks produce, instead, bloody wounds until they are stanched by one with fresh flowers. But Ismene's interpretation shows that Mileta's dream really concerns love and death: "It is a signe you shall fall in loue with hearing faire words. Water signifieth counsell, flowers death. And nothing can purge your louing humour but death" (31-33).

Ismene's own dream is the most obscure of all: "I remember last night but one, I dreamed mine eie tooth was lose, & that I thrust it out with my tonge" (36-37). But Mileta is able to provide a clue to its interpretation when she suggests that the lost tooth signifies the loss of a friend driven away by Ismene's incessant prattling. The dream of Canope clearly has as its theme pretense and riches: "Mee thought I was shadowed with a clowd, where labouring to vnwrap my selfe, I was more intangled. But in the midst of my striuing, it seemed to mysell gold, with faire drops; I filled my lap, and running to shew it my fellowes, it turned to duste, I blushed, they laughed" (56-61). It remains for Ismene, however, to realize its underlying warning and significance; she tells Canope not to let gold tempt her lap lest she then have to blush for shame.

Lamia's dream, like Ismene's, is obscure, concerned apparently with tarantulas and lutes. She imagines that, having been bitten by a tarantula, the music of two lutes tuned to a single key can relieve her distress. But Mileta is able to demonstrate that the dream really has to do with love and marriage, the two lutes signifying marital harmony. Favilla's dream, the last in the series, concerns the power of love to transform hearts from the hardest to the hottest organs:

Mee thought going by the sea side amonge Pebels I sawe one playing with a rounde stone, euer throwing it into the water, when the sunne shined: I asked the name, hee saide, it was called *Abeston*, which being once whotte, would neuer be cold, he gaue it me, and vanished. I forgetting my selfe,

delighted with the fayre showe, woulde alwayes shewe it by candle light,
pull it out in the Sunne, and see howe bright it woulde look in the fire,
where catching heate, nothing could coole it: for anger I threwe it against
the wall, and with the heauing vp of myne arme I waked. (79-87)

Again, Mileta provides the interpretation: "Beware of loue, Fauilla:
for womens hearts are such stones, which warmed by affection, cannot be coold by wisdome" (88-89).

There is no doubt that Lyly is interested in dreams. They appear
in abundance in *Sapho* as well as at crucial moments in *Endimion*.
Like other Elizabethan dramatists, Lyly uses dreams to figure forth
suppressed states of feeling, especially frustrated sexual desire. Of
course, the ladies-in-waiting may never have really experienced
these dreams but fabricated them to please their mistress. But
whether they are real or not is unimportant; what is important is
that Sapho listens to all of the dreams and to their interpretations,
and thus becomes convinced of their universality as well as of their
veracity. She is thus inclined to rely upon them to a greater extent
than she ordinarily would.

In fact, she commands her maidens to cease their talking so that
she can try again to lose herself in dreams: "Cease your talking: for
I would faine sleepe, to see if I can dreame, whether the birde hath
feathers, or the Antes wings" (93-94). The stress on feathers and
wings very obviously suggests a suppressed desire for freedom, a
freedom to love which has been and will continue to be denied
Sapho so far as Phao is concerned. She wants him, wants to love
him, that is clear. The dream, then, serves not only as an avenue
into Sapho's libido but also as a confirmation of her desire.

Act IV, Scene iv, returns to the action where it broke off at Act
IV, Scene ii, 41, as Venus persuades Vulcan to forge new arrows for
Cupid so that he can work on Phao. Although he is aware of Venus's
dissembling, Vulcan grants her wish. In a kind of mock-heroic tone,
Lyly devotes most of Act V, Scene i, to an elaborate description of
Cupid's new arrows—their substance, effects, etc. Some arrows
cause mistrust and jealousy; some, disdain; some, passionate desire,
constancy in love, shrewdness in artifice; others, designed especially
for court ladies, work liking, not love; affability in speech, not faith.

Act V, Scene ii, serves as a *deus ex machina* in that it readjusts
feeling in a way that is neither psychologically consistent nor ap-

propriate to demands of plot. Cupid frees Sapho from her burn-
ing passion for Phao, then causes Phao to despise Venus, but fails
to release Phao from his passion for Sapho. Venus is, of course,
furious at this twist of events; and she threatens her son and Sapho,
who remain unconcerned. From Sapho's point of view, Venus has
been a mighty poor love goddess, a failing she is quick to point out:
"Euery rude asse shall not say he is in loue. It is a toye made for
Ladies, and I will keepe it onely for Ladies" (94-96). Sapho not only
virtually destroys Venus here but also unconsciously reveals her own
prejudices, as well as the eccentricities which characterize Lyly's
comic view of love. Love operates in *Sapho* as it does in
Shakespeare's *Midsummer Night's Dream*: supernatural agencies
are responsible for turning it on and off at will. Puck's "Lord, what
fools these mortals be" can be applied equally well to the characters
in *Sapho*. In neither play is love an emotion deeply rooted in the
psyche—it is rather a superficial emotion that encourages eccentric
behavior. Of all Lyly's plays, excepting *Midas*, of course, *Sapho* is
the least profound in terms of love theory.

The futures of Sapho, Venus, and Cupid having been arranged,
only that of Phao remains. Realizing—and accepting at last—the
impossibility of his situation, Phao decides to leave Syracuse and
return to his oar. The bond which he has established with Sapho
will never be broken: "This shalbe my resolutiõ, where euer I wãder
to be as I were euer kneeling before Sapho, my loyalty vnspotted,
though vnrewarded" (17-19). Phao then returns home, and the play
ends, as Lyly remarked in the "Prologue at the Blackfriars," where
it began.

Lyly remarks also in the "Epilogue" that his play resembles a
labyrinth and that it raises doubts rather than settles issues—a point
which should be considered in regard to the rather uncharacteristic
ending. Although *Sapho* does not end with wedding bells or
marriage feasts, it does, however, raise doubts, rather serious
doubts, in fact, about the total court environment. Lyly is never
enthusiastic about the court, but in *Sapho* he is as virulent as he
ever is in painting a picture of frivolity and mindlessness. The spectacle of Sapho and her ladies parading about consumed in a self-
directed superficiality is the most striking feature of Lyly's play.

CHAPTER 4

Middle Plays

I Gallathea (*Jan. 1, 1587/8*)

LYLY'S *Gallathea* is one of the first Elizabethan comedies to exploit the disguise motif whereby a boy impersonates a girl who pretends to be a boy. The theme of defiance of divinity is developed in a main plot in which Neptune exacts from the inhabitants of North Lincolnshire[1] a tribute: every five years they must offer their fairest maiden to the sea monster, Agar. Tyterus and Melebeus, the fathers of the girls most likely to be sacrificed at the next celebration, disguise their daughters as boys and send them into the forest for security. The girls, each supposing the other to be a boy, meet and fall in love. In the same forest, Cupid plots his revenge on the nymphs of Diana who have defied him: he encourages three of the nymphs to fall in love with the disguised maidens; but when Diana discovers his plot, she sets him to untying love knots as a punishment. Venus manages ultimately to release Cupid from Diana's control by encouraging Neptune, who is in her debt, to forego the tribute. Finally, Venus ensures the happy ending by promising to change one of the girls, disguised as a boy, into a real boy.

Venus is again the practicer, just as she was in *Sapho and Phao*, but with more success this time. She discourages Neptune's tribute and ensures the happy ending. Yet the plot is weak, as is evidenced by the attention paid to three shipwrecked brothers and an alchemist's boy who flourish in a parodic subplot, which has considerable bearing on the main plot: (1) the brothers seek their futures in the forest as do the disguised daughters of Tyterus and Melebeus; (2) the brothers are separated from each other just as the girls are separated from their fathers; (3) the masters whom Rafe serves—alchemist and astronomer—provide a kind of eerie background against which Neptune and the Agar seem less implausible; (4) finally, in bawdy comic language the brothers parody the language of love which appears elsewhere in the play. Although the participants in the main plot and subplot do not meet until the final scene, their careers parallel each other in a refreshingly revealing fashion.

Gallathea represents a third variation on the triangle of love. In *Alexander and Campaspe* two men pursued one woman; in *Sapho and Phao* two women pursued one man; now, in *Gallathea*, all of the participants are women. Not only do Gallathea and Phillida pursue each other, but they are pursued in return by the nymphs of Diana. The resulting triangle has two points constant as the third moves from one nymph to another. The result is a more complex structure, even though Lyly fails to capitalize on the rivalries.

In *Gallathea*, Lyly, like Shakespeare in *The Winter's Tale*, chooses to fool the audience as well as the participants. The audience does not know, nor do the participants, that one of the girls will be changed into a boy; but this information has to be withheld since the confrontations between Gallathea and Phillida are dramatic only because of the impossibility of their situation. If the audience knew that a solution was close at hand, the dramatic tension would quickly drain away. Actually, Lyly plays a trick on the audience by apparently allowing it to share in the truth and to make it feel secure in the knowledge that it is enjoying the spectacle of two girls each of whom is disguised as a boy and who believes the other to be in fact a boy.

But because he chooses to fool everyone, Lyly sacrifices one of the most dramatic elements of disguise—self-knowledge. In mature comedies involving disguise, such as in *Much Ado About Nothing*, characters, by pretending to be someone else, learn something about themselves. By pretending to be someone else, they often discover who they are. Disguise thus leads to self-discovery, and this is one of the most subtle devices a dramatist can employ. Lyly fails, however, to realize the possibilities of the device. How, after all, can a girl disguised as a boy learn about herself when she, in fact, isn't? To become one's opposite offers interesting psychological possibilities, but not in *Gallathea*.

In *Gallathea*, Lyly is moving in a new direction that is destined to take him further and further from traditional Roman comic form and closer to today's Theater of the Absurd. There is something inherently absurd about disguises and the denial of identity which they imply. To disguise one's self is to deny one's individuality, to dislocate one's place in the scheme of things. It is to create, momentarily at least, a topsy-turvy universe in which appearance overcomes reality. This theme of absurdity in *Gallathea* is also developed at the end of the play.

This is not to suggest that Lyly is a sixteenth-century Samuel Beckett, Eugene Ionesco, or Arthur Adamov, for he is not. Although annihilation is devoutly to be wished in many plays that belong to the Theater of the Absurd, just as it is by one of the girls in *Gallathea*, the motive is significantly different. To deny the uniqueness of human personality is to deny that life has meaning. So it is for Beckett, but not for Lyly. Character is denied in *Gallathea* not because it is unreal or meaningless but because without character transformation sexual fulfillment is impossible. Love triumphs whatever the cost to plot or to characterization.

The characters in *Gallathea* are even more lightly sketched than are the characters in *Campaspe* and *Sapho*. Gallathea and Phillida are almost indistinguishable, except that the former would not willingly defy destiny. It is important for Lyly's purposes that Gallathea and Phillida are not sharply individualized. Since one of them will be changed into a boy at the end of the play, neither can display a strong personality since that personality will be annihilated.

Despite problems of characterization, Peter Saccio still finds *Gallathea* to be "the most perfectly executed and the most luminously clear of Lyly's plays. It is an exquisite work of art."[2] Saccio concludes his introduction to *Gallathea* by suggesting that

Lyly's dramaturgy has become more sinuous, more suggestive, and less intellectually rigid. The juxtaposed scenes create a series of internal echoes, parallels, and balanced contrasts that dance forward with expanded meaning and rhythm. The central movement forward is the exfoliation of the central figures of the gods. . . . In short, allegorical dramaturgy has in *Campaspe* the multilinear power of a child's connect-the-dots design: given the dots, dramatic action reveals the proper structure that intricately ties them into a firm whole. Allegorical dramaturgy has in *Gallathea* a more organic power, the expanding power of opening blossoms: given the buds, dramatic action reveals the depths that lie within.[3]

Lyly's growing command of dramatic techniques is illustrated in the opening scene of *Gallathea* as Tyterus lectures his daughter, Gallathea, about the difficulties of their situation. Although Tyterus has considerable to say, Lyly does not assign to him a long speech; he uses interruptions from Gallathea to break up the speech into short, dramatic bursts. Tyterus's speech provides motivation for Gallathea's disguise, lowers a veil of darkness on the proceedings by referring to the ceremony of human sacrifice, and introduces the overriding theme of attempted defiance of divinity.

Variety is essential to the success of Lyly's comedies. *Sapho* falters because too much attention is focused on the three principal characters, but Lyly avoids such a narrow focus in *Gallathea*, just as he did in *Campaspe*. After introducing the first of the two father-daughter combinations in Act I, Scene i, Lyly switches in Scene ii to a new set of characters, Cupid and a nymph of Diana, and to a new intrigue. Cupid's attempt to win the nymph to the ways of love is met with a refusal couched in such Hubristic terms that retribution is bound to follow. Cupid takes advantage of the opportunity to offer a definition of love: "A heate full of coldnesse, a sweet full of bitternesse, a paine ful of pleasantnesse; which maketh thoughts haue eyes, and harts eares; bred by desire, nursed by delight, weaned by ielousie, kild by dissembling, buried by ingratitude; and this is loue!" (16-19). Cupid has apparently been reading *Euphues and His England*: "You see what Love is—begun with grief, continued with sorrow, ended with death; a pain full of pleasure, a joy replenished with misery, a Heaven, a Hell, a God, a Devil, and what not" (285).

The action of Act I, Scene i, is repeated in Act I, Scene iii, with a second father-daughter combination. Like Tyterus, Melebeus is concerned for the safety of his daughter, Phillida; and he disguises her as a boy. In contrast to Gallathea, Phillida is an obliging young lady who objects to nothing her father proposes. Like Gallathea, however, she is somewhat concerned about the possible moral implications of her disguise: "For then I must keepe companie with boyes, and commit follies vnseemelie for my sexe; or keepe company with girles, and be thought more wanton then becommeth me" (17-19). But her concerns are soothed over by her father's comforting words.

Rafe, Robin, and Dick, the three brothers, are introduced in Act I, Scene iv. In the composition of his subplot, Lyly remains within the tradition of Roman comedy: the three brothers are the equivalent of the three sons of Sylvius in *Campaspe* and of Molus and Cryticus in *Sapho and Phao*. Witty apprentices, pages, and servants display their wares throughout Lyly's plays, always with the same unflagging zest and vitality. In *Endimion*, they make a fool of Sir Thopas; in *Midas*, they gull Motto; in *Mother Bombie*, they trick the four crusty fathers; and they are absent only from *The Woman in the Moon* and *Loves Metamorphosis*. Their wit inevitably vanquishes meanness and penury of spirit. In *Gallathea*, however, they do more than merely add variety; they function in a plot that parodies the main plot. The main theme of defiance of divinity, as Peter Saccio points out, is worked out against a backdrop of violence and savagery.[4] In the subplot, however, the same theme is advanced without savagery and violence. The astronomer and alchemist, like the fathers and their daughters, are trying to defy divinity. They seek knowledge or power that is beyond them and, in the process, make themselves ridiculous.

Rafe, Robin, and Dick survive a shipwreck and, accompanied by the mariner, arrive in Lincolnshire. Failing to master the mariner's compass, they occasion the mariner's scorn. But in condemning the brothers, the mariner condemns himself by his display of braggadocio: "I can shift the Moone and the Sunne, and know by one Carde, what all you cannot do by a whole payre. The Lodestone that alwaies holdeth his nose to the North, the two and thirty poynts for the winde, the wonders I see woulde make all you blinde: you be but boyes, I feare the Sea no more then a dish of water. Why fooles, it is but a liquid element" (30-35). Such presumption as this links the mariner, the alchemist, and the astronomer to the main plot.

Having been discharged by the mariner, the three brothers agree to separate to seek their fortunes; but they do so with the proviso that they will meet again after a year has passed. The scene ends with a song in which they express their discontentment with the sea and in which they refer to themselves as "*Neptune's* slaves" (86), thus establishing an additional link with the main story.

Structurally, the second act is similar to the first. In the first scene, Lyly presents the two disguised girls along with Diana and her nymphs; in the second, Cupid and Neptune. Then Lyly varies the pattern. The first act closed with the three brothers; in the second act, the brothers are presented in the third scene, along with the alchemist; and the act ends with two short scenes devoted to the disguised girls. Juxtaposition of scenes, then, remains the basic dramatic technique.

The first of a series of confrontations between Gallathea and Phillida occurs in Act II, Scene i. Unfortunately, these confrontations are flaccid because Lyly fails to exploit the dramatic potential of a situation that is unusual. Lyly presents a spectacle of two boy actors impersonating girls; and what is wrong with the situation, of course, is that the participants are of the same sex. The theme of appearance and reality, which serves Lyly so well in other plays, is here relatively useless. Deception is present, obviously, but it works against the comic resolution since the girls have no real recourse to human solutions. Humanly speaking, their situation is impossible; and their encounters reflect, therefore, the static quality of their predicament. For example, Gallathea and Phillida are brought together but are not allowed to react emotionally to each other. Instead of engaging each other in face-to-face confrontations, they complain, in asides to the audience, about the unseemliness of their situation.

The disguise motif increases momentum in Act II, Scene ii, when Cupid, intent upon the revenge scheme he announced in Act I, Scene ii, disguises himself as a girl and lets his arrows fly at the nymphs of Diana. Neptune, who has observed Cupid's actions, now joins the game by disguising himself as a shepherd so that he may "marke all, and in the end will marre all" (24).

Act II, Scene iii, picks up the action where it ended in Act I, Scene iv. Having failed to realize his fortune, Rafe meets Peter, the alchemist's helper, and is captivated by his stories about the alchemist's art. The stories are, as one discovers later, strictly for Rafe's benefit; for Peter, who has grown sick of alchemy, is looking for a substitute for himself. Lyly puts into the mouth of the alchemist a scientific jargon drawn from alchemical terms of the day: "An ounce of Siluer limde, as much of crude Mercury, of

Spirits foure, beeing tempered with the bodies seauen, by multiplying of it ten times, comes for one pound, eyght thousand pounds, so
that I may haue onely Beechen coales" (75-78). The alchemist is, of
course, another example of a character who attempts to defy divinity; but he never succeeds in making gold. Act II, Scene iii is
noteworthy also in that it is the first scene in which Lyly presents
fairies on the stage, the little people who appear again in *Endimion*
and who reach their apogee in Shakespeare's *A Midsummer Night's
Dream.*

The second act concludes with two parallel scenes: the first involves Gallathea; the second, Phillida. Each girl laments her unfortunate position and what she believes to be her unrequited love. By
Act III, Scene i, Cupid has enacted his revenge. Diana's nymphs are
now in love with Gallathea (disguised as Tyterus) and Phillida
(disguised as Melebeus). Telusa loves Phillida-Melebeus, Eurota
loves Gallathea-Tyterus, as does Ramia, who confesses that all of
the nymphs are in love, the effect of which is described by Eurota:
"I feele my thoughts vnknit, mine eyes vnstaied, my hart I know
not how affected, or infected, my sleepes broken and full of
dreames, my wakenesse sad and full of sighes, my selfe in all
thinges vnlike my selfe" (46-49).

Love in *Gallathea* is, then, a disturbing, unsettling phenomenon,
but Lyly fails to capitalize on it. The audience is denied the spectacle of lovers brought face-to-face in comic encounters, or even
brought together in animated discussions about love. Instead, Lyly
uses his characters as spokesmen for various attitudes about love. In
Act III, Scene i, for example, Telusa and Eurota voice a mild
Neoplatonic attitude in their insistence upon the importance of the
ears and eyes in the experience of love; but no dramatic exchange
occurs between these characters and others—no tension results from
opposed attitudes toward love. Instead, Lyly presents, in short, a
brief explication of a doctrine of love, not a dramatic presentment of
what Neoplatonic love is like, or what it is like to be in love.

In Act III, Scene ii, the disguises begin to fall away as Gallathea
and Phillida suspect the truth about each other. Act III, Scene iii,
returns to Rafe, now disenchanted with his master, the alchemist. In
this scene he trades him for a new master, an astronomer, who has
enthralled Rafe with his "science." Lyly has great sport in *Gallathea*
with Elizabethan pseudoscience at the expense of astronomers and

alchemists, whose "learned" jargon is not so far removed from actual "scientific" vocabulary of the time or, for that matter, of any time.[5]

Disguises continue to fall away in Act III, Scene iv, as Diana pierces the disguise of Cupid and realizes that he is a god. After sending for Cupid, Diana delivers a lengthy speech castigating her nymphs for deserting her in favor of Venus. Use "the needle for Samplers," she says, not "the penne for Sonets" (48), an injunction which, according to R. W. Bond, reflects Queen Elizabeth's disapproval of marriages among her courtiers.[6] Diana's criticism is not directed against marriage, however, but against love which was quite a different matter in royal circles. Diana reveals her unfamilarity with love in her approach to the subject for she tries to level reasonable arguments against it. But, as one of Diana's nymphs, Ramia, points out, love is beyond reason; logic is not to the point.

When Cupid finally arrives, Diana threatens to torture him unless he performs a different task for her each day. When he counter-threatens in the name of Venus, Diana ignores his threats. Lyly interrupts this episode just long enough to remind the audience that Neptune is about to claim his sacrifice (IV.i); then he returns immediately to Cupid, now helplessly bound by Diana's nymphs, who sing a triumphal song over him. The song not only entertains in its own right but also is a linking motif between Act IV, Scene i, and Act IV, Scene ii. It parallels the human sacrifice demanded by Neptune: ". . . see torn/The boy in pieces" (3-4). After the song, Cupid, under compulsion, agrees to untie the love knots which have bound the nymphs and to study how he can better serve Diana.

At this point, Lyly again inserts a short scene in order to remind the audience of the human sacrifice that serves as a backdrop for much of the action in *Gallathea*. In Act IV, Scene iii, Neptune, conscious of the deception practiced on him by Tyterus and Melebeus, strikes an ominous note:

Thys day is the solemne Sacrifice at thys Tree, wherein the fairest virgine (were not the inhabitants faithlesse) should be offered vnto me, but so ouer carefull are Fathers to their children, that they forgette the safetie of their Countrey, & fearing to become vnnaturall, become vnreasonable: their slights may bleere men, deceiue me they cannot; I wil be here at the houre, and shew as great crueltie as they haue doone craft, & well shall they know that *Neptune* should haue beene intreated, not cosened. (1-8)

The first face-to-face confrontation between Gallathea and Phillida occurs in Act IV, Scene iv. Convinced that the other is actually a girl disguised as a boy, each tries to trap the other into a confession. The exchange that ensues can hardly be called a battle of wits, but the participants are at least brought into a potentially dramatic relationship. There is also an undercurrent of eroticism, however unusual, that lends substance to this encounter. Gallathea and Phillida are in love—and with each other! Lyly has taken the traditional Roman formula of two nubile youngsters separated by some obstacle, usually a pimp or older suitor, and driven it to its extreme limits. In *Gallathea*, two young lovers are separated by an obstacle that is unique in English literary history—both lovers are girls! If natural sexual fulfillment is to ensue, an unnatural agency has to be invoked, which is, of course, precisely what happens.

First, however, Lyly offers a parodic commentary on the main love intrigue as Rafe, reunited with his brother Robin, explains, with bawdy innuendo, the occupation of an alchemist:

RAFFE.   What Robin? what newes? what fortune?
ROBIN.   Faith I haue had but badde fortune, but I prie-thee tell me thine.
RAFFE.   I have had two Maisters, not by arte but by nature; one sayd, that by multiplying he woulde make a penny tenne pound.
ROBIN.   I but coulde he doe it?
RAFFE.   Could he doe it quoth you? why man, I sawe a prettie wench come to his shoppe, where with puffing, blowing, and sweating, he so plyed her, that hee multiplyed her.
ROBIN.   Howe?
RAFFE.   Why he made her of one, two.
ROBIN.   What by fire?
RAFFE.   No, by the Philosophers stone.[7]
ROBIN.   Why, haue Philosophers such stones?
RAFFE.   I, but they lie in a priuie cupboord. (V.i.13-26)

This bawdy conversation serves a dual function. First, through it the response of the audience to the love between Gallathea and Phillida is made more complex. By moving from the naturalistic sex described by Rafe to the erotic predicament of the young lovers, Lyly adds depth to what would otherwise remain wish-fulfillment. The audience is vividly reminded that there is more to sex than pretty speeches and desperate longings. There is something basic about it, which involves, as Rafe puts it, "puffing, blowing, and sweating." Second, this speech recalls the audience to the theme which the alchemist and astronomer served to illustrate earlier—the defiance of divinity. In this capacity the scene thus links the main love story and the parodic subplot in still another way.

The penultimate scene (V.ii) prepares for the comic denouement by presenting still another variation on the theme just discussed. Attempting to deceive Neptune, the people select Haebe as their sacrificial offering. Since she is unattractive, she is understandably upset at the selection and registers her concern in a forty-seven-line aria. The Agar, who sees that she is ugly, refuses to claim her as Neptune's victim. Instead of rejoicing in her salvation, Haebe is indignant at being refused. Vanity, thy name is woman!

In the last scene, all of the characters are on stage for the first time. Gallathea and Phillida enter, still maintaining their disguises; and they retire as Neptune enters, raging about the deceptions that have been practiced on him. Then Diana and Venus appear, and Venus seeks justice for Diana's enslavement of Cupid. The goddesses put their case before Neptune, who finds himself in the uncomfortable position of settling a dispute between goddesses of equal rank. Recognizing the need for compromise, Neptune agrees to stop his victimization of virgins if Diana will return Cupid to Venus, his mother. When Tyterus and Melebeus enter, accompanied by Galathea and Phillida, Venus consents to transform one of the girls into a boy (one does not know which—it really does not matter), and everyone leaves for the church where the wedding will take place. There they are joined by Rafe, Robin, and Dick who at last are able to fill their bellies with "Capons rumpes, or some such daintie dishes" (197).

According to *Gallathea*'s latest editor, Anne Lancashire, the happy ending is an ironic comment on love, self-deception, and reality: "Given man's physical nature, and his capacity for self-deception, harmony and happiness will come to him only by chance. The synthesis of reason and passion, head and heart, reality and dream, represented in V.iii by the coming together of all plot strands, is

elusive indeed, and to be achieved only by luck, and only momentarily, in life as in the play's wedding feast (which we do not see)."[8]

Considered in relation to Gallathea and Phillida, this critical view
has much to recommend it. The lovers are ultimately reconciled by
something resembling chance. But to maintain this view is to argue
against the complexity of Lyly's vision, since chance, a parody of
destiny, creates confusion rather than complexity. Lyly's fictive universe, whether in *Gallathea* or in *Euphues*, is built on the premise
that perception, although difficult to achieve, is possible. Chance,
however, destroys the possibility of perception and, therefore,
shatters the mirror which Lyly holds up to life.

Except for the unusual obstacle posed by two lovers of the same
sex, *Gallathea* conforms to what many critics regard as comic form.
Not only is the erotic impulse satisfied, but a new society is also
formed at the end of the drama. The devious methods of the older
generation, represented by Tyterus and Melebeus—not to mention
the astronomer and alchemist—are replaced by the sincerity
and forthrightness of the younger generation, represented by
Gallathea, Phillida, and the three brothers. The savagery suggested
by the human-sacrifice motif dissolves into gaiety as the gods and
goddesses compromise, with the result that bloodthirstiness and
anger give way to the fruits of love. Finally, not chance but love
brought about by compromise paves the way to bliss.

II Endimion (*Feb. 2, 1587/8*)

Endimion is Lyly's comedy of ideas. Except for some antics, the
play offers little action: Dipsas casts a spell, Eumenides journeys to
a strange land, Endimion falls asleep, and Corsites is pinched black-
and-blue by fairies. There is some slapstick and horseplay, but the
comedy is basically an abstract drama which explores the relationships of five different groups of characters. The effect of love on
human character provides the stimulus, and the analysis of love in
five of its many faces forms the substance of the comedy. *Endimion*
is by far the most leisurely examination of love that the drama of the
1580's produced.[9]

Endimion, a courtly lover, loves Cynthia, the Moon Goddess;
Tellus, the Earth Goddess, loves Endimion; and Corsites, a plain
soldier, loves Tellus. Around this network Lyly weaves a complex

tale of magic and folklore. Tellus, in revenge for being spurned by Endimion, arranges for the sorceress Dipsas to place a spell on Endimion which causes him to sleep eternally. Cynthia dispatches messengers to various exotic lands to find a cure, but only Endimion's friend Eumenides is successful in finding one. A magic fountain, to which he is permitted access because of his friendship with Endimion, reveals that Endimion can be awakened by a kiss from Cynthia. A parodic subplot exists in the person of Sir Tophas, a foolish knight, whose actions parallel those of Endimion.[10]

Unfortunately, this play has attracted critics who delight in predicating topical parallels between the characters in the play and real personages in the court of Queen Elizabeth. From N.J. Halpin's *Oberon's Vision* in 1843 to J. W. Bennett's "Oxford and Endimion" in 1942,[11] one learned conjecture after another has been entertained. For Halpin, Endimion and Corsites represent the Earl of Leicester and Sir Edward Stafford; for Bennett, they stand for the Earl of Oxford and Sir Henry Lee.[12] Fortunately, recent criticism has shied away from historical allegory in favor of more literary types. Bernard Huppé, for example, argues that if *Endimion* is an allegory, "it deals with the mental and psychological world of being: relations in it are relations of ideas and states."[13] For Huppé, Cynthia represents not Queen Elizabeth, but Virtuous Love; Tellus represents not Mary Queen of Scots, but Earthly Passion.[14]

Endimion is the most frequently anthologized of Lyly's plays, and therefore the one most familiar to students of Elizabethan drama. It is, however, atypical. With the exception of *Mother Bombie*, also atypical, *Endimion* is approximately twenty-five percent longer than Lyly's other plays; and it is more complex, expecially more complex than the comedies which precede it. *Alexander and Campaspe* and *Sapho and Phao* are basically single-plot dramas, even though Diogenes's story in *Campaspe* tends toward independent coexistence; *Gallathea* has a clearly developed subplot, but one which is relegated to the background (the three brothers appear in five of the twenty scenes). Not only is the main plot in *Endimion* more complex but the subplots are also more heavily stressed (Sir Tophas alone appears in six of the seventeen scenes).

Endimion has a dramatic structure that is extremely balanced. The supernatural sleep of Endimion and his subsequent awakening are used by Lyly as focal points for the action. Endimion falls asleep at the end of the second act and awakens at the end of the fourth. The period before his sleep consists of two acts of seven scenes, five of which are devoted to Endimion and two to Sir Tophas; the period during his sleep consists of two acts of seven scenes, two of which are devoted to Endimion and five to the subplots (actually there is some overlapping here, but the scheme remains valid). The second division, with its emphasis on the subplots, thus inverts the first division, as indeed it must since Endimion is asleep through most of the third and fourth acts. The final division, after Endimion awakens, consists of one act of three scenes: the first is devoted to Endimion; the second, to Sir Tophas; the third, to a denouement which unifies all of the stories.

Endimion is Lyly's *Hamlet*. No historical or allegorical approach satisfies more than a few critics; the ending shrouds the play in ambiguity; and there are so many fashionable topics that every man finds something of interest. Always quick to capitalize on current interests, Lyly outdoes himself in *Endimion* by fastening upon themes and topics that were the rage in fashionable society, such as mutability (I.i), art versus nature (I.iv, II.iii), black versus white magic (II.iii, V.i). The two controlling themes, however, reach back in history, one to Classical antiquity and the other to the late Middle Ages: friendship and romantic love are what *Endimion* is all about.

In the Prologue to *Endimion*, Lyly appears to be establishing a critical principle when he writes: "Wee present neither Comedie, nor Tragedie, nor storie, nor anie thing, but that whosoever heareth may say this, Why heere is a tale of the Man in the Moone" (8-10). That *Endimion* is not a tragedy is obvious; no one dies, and death is essential to Elizabethan tragedy. That it is not a comedy is not so obvious. Perhaps Lyly has in mind the ending, which, far from bestowing blessings in true comic fashion, is a mixed bag of responses. Although Endimion regains his youth, he does not get Cynthia—and to serve by standing and waiting is an uncomfortable position for a lover. Eumenides gets his heart's desire—Semele, a sharp-tongued, shrewish female who will make the connubial bed a noisy place indeed. Corsites gets Tellus, the professional troublemaker. Dipsas and Bagoa are reunited, but far too late, for life has already passed them by. Perhaps of all the lovers, only Sir Tophas will not be disenchanted with his bargain. He asks for little,

and little is what he gets. The irony which undercuts the love senti-
ment in the play is summarized in Sir Tophas's description of his
ideal woman: "Turne her to a true loue or false, so shee be a wench
I care not" (V.iii. 279-280). Behind Sir Tophas's nonchalance lies a
cynical antidote to the various love theories which appear, however
diluted, in *Endimion*—God made them male and female, and *vive
la différence!*

The ending, then, does not conform to expectation. Although
wedding bells ring, their sound is muted. A new society is formed,
but there is some doubt that it will be superior to the old. J. W. H.
Atkins argues that Lyly, although indebted to Roman comedy, rejects the rigidity of Classical drama; and Lyly, in refusing to classify
his plays as comedies or tragedies, denies that the boundaries of
dramatic form have been permanently fixed.[15] It is possible that
Lyly thought of himself as a reformer, but to credit Atkins's argument is to posit a dramatic form more rigidly established than the
one that in fact existed in the Elizabethan era. The whole history of
the period is one of experimentation and change, from the early
rhymed couplets of Nicholas Udall to the finely chiseled prose of
Ben Jonson, from the heavy prosody of Robert Greene to the exquisite blank verse of Shakespeare. From *Ralph Roister Doister* to
The Winter's Tale is a long journey indeed.

The principal theme in *Endimion* concerns the convention of
male friendship. It not only serves as a framework, much as
Shakespeare uses it in *The Merchant of Venice*, but also links
together many of the diverse plot elements, such as Endimion's
sleep and Eumenides's excursion into the desert. This theme is
revealed through action as well as through dialogue; for example,
Eumenides apparently sacrifices his own happiness for the sake of
his friend Endimion when he encounters the magic fountain in Act
III, Scene iv. Generally, however, themes and issues are revealed
through debate; and action is sacrificed to witty exchanges of
dialogue. The wit, however, is non-dramatic; for no change in
character or situation results. In Act I, Scene i, for example, the confrontation between Endimion and Eumenides is non-dramatic.
Nothing that Eumenides says in any way changes Endimion; in
fact, all of Eumenides's objections could have been anticipated by
Endimion in a soliloquy. Lyly does reveal a sense for the dramatic,
however, by presenting the exposition in dialogue form.

The opening scene establishes premises upon which the drama is built. The stage is set for comedy as Endimion's romantic inclinations have been thwarted: boy has met girl, boy wants girl, but boy cannot have girl. There is, in *Endimion*, an even greater obstacle than is found in previous plays. In *Campaspe*, the obstacle was a wealthier suitor, Alexander the Great; in *Sapho and Phao*, the obstacle was social—queens do not marry ferrymen, however attractive they might be; in *Gallathea*, the obstacle was sexual—both lovers were girls; in *Endimion*, the obstacle is celestial—Endimion is literally in love with the moon!

The conflict which evolves from Act I, Scene i, is between what is desirable and what is possible—between the aspirations of Endimion, which are "stitched to the starres" (5), and those of Eumenides, "which creepe on the earth" (73-74). Eumenides's function in this scene is to serve as commentator on the impossibility of Endimion's quest. Such absolutes as Endimion seeks are unattainable in life, says Eumenides—man must compromise. Unable to understand or appreciate Endimion's longing, Eumenides believes that he has fallen prey either to moon madness or to melancholy.

Repetition with variation characterizes Act I, Scene ii. The nondramatic debate technique is again employed as Tellus and Floscula take the places of Endimion and Eumenides. Just as is the case with Eumenides earlier in the play, Floscula is present for convenience's sake; her criticisms, like those of Eumenides, could have been anticipated by Tellus in a soliloquy. Furthermore, the second scene opens with the speech of a lover and ends with the speech of a critic, just as did the first scene. Finally, both scenes present identical situations in which a character, lamenting an unrequited love, is criticized by a confidant. Although the situations are identical, the tone is sharply differentiated: Endimion will be satisfied with nothing less than possession of the goddess herself, but Tellus will settle for the appearance of love—"It shall suffice me if the world talke that I am fauoured of *Endimion*" (73-74).

Superficially, Act I, Scene ii, presents a situation common in a love triangle when the jilted female plots revenge. But Tellus is not an ordinary female—she is, in fact, the earth goddess: "No comparison *Floscula?* and why so? is not my beauty diuine, whose body is decked with faire flowers, and vaines are Vines, yeelding sweet liquor to the dullest spirits, whose eares are Corne, to bring strength, and whose heares are grasse, to bring abundance? Doth not Frankinsence & Myrrhe breath out of my nostrils, and all the sacrifice of the Gods breede in my bowels? Infinite are my creatures, without which neyther thou, nor *Endimion*, nor any could loue, or liue" (19-26).

But Tellus wants to play the part of a Petrarchan heroine: "His sharp wit . . . shall hee vse, in flattering of my face, and deuising Sonnets in my fauour" (56-58). Her concluding speech reinforces the passionate craving of love already implied: "*Floscula*, they that be so poore that they haue neyther nette nor hooke, will rather poyson dowe then pyne with hunger: and she that is so opprest with loue, that shee is neyther able with beauty nor wit to obtaine her freende, wyll rather vse vnlawfull meanes, then try vntollerable paines" (78-82).

There is a nice irony in the opening two scenes. As Endimion plots his attack on Cynthia, Tellus plots her counterattack on Endimion. Furthermore, just as Endimion's desire to possess Cynthia is to be frustrated, so is Tellus's desire to possess Endimion. Both attempt to upset the natural order of the universe—Endimion by aspiring beyond his station; Tellus by employing Floscula to destroy a normal human inclination, love. Finally, Tellus's solution to the paradox she formulates—"Loth I am *Endimion* thou shouldest die, because I loue thee well; and that thou shouldest liue it greeueth mee, because thou louest *Cynthia* too well. In these extremities what shall I doe?" (35-38)—is itself an unnatural solution: "He shall neyther liue, nor die" (39). This unnaturalness is made explicit by Floscula's reaction to it: "A reuenge incredible, and if it may be, vnnatural" (52).

To this point in the drama, the situation has been serious, even grim. But now (I.iii) Lyly introduces burlesque in the form of Sir Tophas, originally Pyrgopolynices in Plautus's *Miles Gloriosus* and more recently Ralph in *Ralph Roister Doister*. (Lyly's braggart soldier differs from these predecessors in that he does not profess to be a great lover; in this respect, his literary precedent is Chaucer's Sir Thopas.) The true wit of the pages, Dares and Samias, is contrasted with the false wit of Tophas. The debate technique of the first two scenes is dropped in favor of a mock-heroic approach characterized by a great disparity between words and situation. Tophas's ridiculousness is quickly established by his handling of the fine art of definition. Asked to define a poet, Tophas replies, "Why foole, a Poet is as much as one shoulde say, a Poet" (17). As a university man, Tophas serves as a target for the barbs of not only Dares and Samias but every other intelligent being as well. There is unquestionably much of Lyly's own anti-academic prejudice incorporated in this play. His own dissatisfaction with the curriculum at Oxford was well known and probably had some bearing on the academic satire in *Endimion*.[16]

More important than his inability to define intelligently is Tophas's inability to distinguish between appearance and reality. He imagines that wrens are as dangerous as eagles and would hunt them with a blunderbuss. Like his successor, Sir John Falstaff, Tophas reacts to situations in an exaggerated and absurd fashion. But whereas Falstaff frequently exaggerates for effect, Tophas does it naturally.

Although not himself a lover, Tophas's opening line—"I brooke not thys idle humor of loue, it tickleth not my lyuer, . . ." (7-8)—mocks the earlier love themes and prepares for the retribution that love later exacts from Tophas. In this way, as well as by paralleling the careers of Tophas and Endimion, Lyly unifies the two stories. The Tophas story, however, does function as an independent unit until the end of the play when it is integrated with the main story. For the sake of psychological plausibility, Lyly has to keep the Tophas story separate, since its mock-heroic tone of absurdity and ridiculousness does not harmonize with the grim seriousness that characterizes the Endimion story.

A new danger to Endimion is introduced in Act I, Scene iv, in the form of the sorceress Dipsas. Her magical powers are clearly spelled out—she can darken the sun and remove the moon from its course (20-21). The one thing she cannot do, however, is control love. Although she can weaken its force, she cannot destroy it; and, perhaps more importantly, she cannot rule hearts—she cannot make Endimion love Tellus. The debate technique is used more dramatically here than earlier; characters change under the force of opposing ideas, and stubbornness yields to cooperation as, for the first time in the comedy, one character consents to act on behalf of another.

Act II marks a turning point in the action when Endimion and Tellus are brought together in a face-to-face encounter. The conflict, which until now has been abstract, is made concrete as it is embedded in the clash of human personalities. Endimion's opening soliloquy (II.i), although far too long to be dramatically effective, develops his role as lover. Complaining that for seven long years he has played the role to the hilt, he enumerates his symptoms: "Beholde my sad teares, my deepe sighes, my hollowe eyes, my broken sleepes, my heauie countenaunce" (11-12). Endimion has been suffering as every Courtly lover ought to suffer: "Every lover regularly turns pale in the presence of his beloved. . . .When a lover suddenly catches sight of his beloved his heart palpitates. . . . He whom the thought of love vexes, eats and sleeps very little."[17]

The encounter between Endimion and Tellus is dramatic—she lays a trap; he falls into it, thus confirming her suspicions that he only pretends to love her. The trap itself depends on two factors for success, verbal wit and urgency. Lyly employs the rhetorical device of stichomythia (dialogue delivered in alternating lines) effectively as Tellus leads Endimion into making admissions against his will simply because the cut and thrust of the dialogue do not give him time to compose his thoughts. In revealing his affection for Cynthia, Endimion violates the code of secrecy, an integral part of the Courtly Love tradition; and for this violation he pays dearly.

Act II, Scene ii, is divided into two parts: (1) a quarrel between Scintilla and Favilla, and (2) the gulling of Sir Tophas. The quarrel, which has little relevance to the play as a whole, may simply reflect an actual quarrel between two of Elizabeth's ladies-in-waiting. Dares, however, provides a unifying link, however tenuous, with his realistic remarks about love: "How say you *Fauilla,* is not loue a lurcher, that taketh mens stomacks away that they cannot eate, their spleene that they cannot laugh, their harts that they cannot fight, theyr eyes that they cannot sleepe, and leaueth nothing but lyuers to make nothing but Louers?" (9-13).

The second part of this scene (57-156) repeats ideas and attitudes introduced earlier, especially in Act I, Scene iii, but Lyly handles them more dramatically by embodying them in the two ladies-in-waiting. Sir Tophas's anti-romantic tendencies now appear in a concrete situation, and they have as their object the ladies whose business is to be expert in affairs of the heart. In its entirety, Act II,

Scene ii, also serves to create tension by delaying the revenge of Tellus.

The first part of Act II, Scene iii (1-23), repeats the opening of Act II, Scene i, and culminates in the symbolic death of Endimion, a motif adopted by Lyly from Udall's *Ralph Roister Doister,* [18] when he falls asleep on a lunary bank. The revenge of Tellus completed, the last part of Act II, Scene iii, recapitulates arguments directed against the unnaturalness of the revenge. In short, magic is being used for improper ends!

Endimion's sleep concludes the first major movement in the play. During the two acts that Endimion sleeps, the dramatic focus shifts to the search for a remedy for his illness. Here, at what is roughly the middle of the play, the hero's fortunes are at their nadir, as they generally are at this point in most comedies. What follows in the last three acts provides a partial restoration. Actually, the first movement concludes with a dumb show, a visual representation of the dream which Endimion explicates upon awakening in the last act.

The new movement initiated in Act III, Scene i, is signaled by the appearance of new characters—Cynthia, Semele, Corsites, Panelion, and Zontes. The initial exchange between Semele and Eumenides follows:

SEM.   It were good *Eumenides* that you tooke a nappe with your friend, for your speech beginneth to be heauy.
EUM.   Contrarie to your nature, *Semele*, which hath beene alwaies accounted light. (12-15)

This exchange contains just enough wit to annoy Cynthia, who orders its immediate cessation. However, a more serious breach of decorum is occasioned by Tellus's tactlessness in suggesting that Cynthia's judgment of Endimion falls somewhat short of the mark. This imprudent remark results in Tellus's exile and prepares for the subsequent scene (III.ii). One's initial view of Cynthia confirms what one has already learned about her in the first two acts: she is dignified, orderly, compassionate, but, when aroused, authoritarian in the extreme. The scene closes with Eumenides being dispatched to Thessaly, Zontes to Greece, and Panelion to Egypt, to find a remedy for Endimion's sleeping sickness. In order to make credible the time required for such journeys, Lyly now devotes his attention to Tellus and Tophas.

Since Cynthia can do little besides await the news from her messengers, since Endimion can do nothing at all, and since the Sir Tophas story will not bear much weight, Lyly introduces a new complication in Act III, Scene ii—the love of Corsites for Tellus. Corsites, a soldier who is aware of the tender side of life, now emerges as an obvious contrast to Sir Tophas; he also emerges, less obviously perhaps, as a parallel to Endimion, for both men pursue one-sided love affairs. Tellus's character continues to degenerate. Like Milton's Satan, she would rather reign in Hell than serve in Heaven: "*Corsites*, there is no sweeter musicke to the miserable then dispayre; and therefore the more bitternesse I feele, the more sweetnes I find; for so vaine were liberty, and so vnwelcome the following of higher fortune, that I chuse rather to pine in this Castle, then to be a Prince in any other Court." (11-15). Both Sir Tophas and Tellus suffer from overweening pride; but, whereas he exemplifies its ridiculousness, she exemplifies its viciousness.

In Act III, Scene iii, Sir Tophas joins the growing list of unrequited lovers, now consisting of Endimion, Eumenides, and Corsites, not to mention Tellus. Love's revenge is complete when Tophas succumbs to the dubious charms of Dipsas. His description of her ought to remind one of Endimion's description of Cynthia, not, of course, in its physical details but in the awe and enthusiasm with which it is delivered:

O what a fine thin hayre hath *Dispsas!* What a prettie low forehead! What a tall & statelie nose! What little hollowe eyes! What great and goodly lypes! Howe harmlesse shee is beeing toothlesse! Her fingers fatte and short, adorned with long nayles like a Bytter! In howe sweete a proportion her cheekes hang downe to her brests like dugges, and her pappes to her waste like bagges! What a lowe stature shee is, and yet what a great foote shee carryeth! Howe thrifty must she be in whom there is no waste! Howe vertuous is shee like to be, ouer whom no man can be ielous! (52-60).

That the description is meant to be humorous is obvious; that it is meant to parody sixteenth-century ideas about feminine beauty is equally obvious.[19]

Further parallelism between Tophas and Endimion is reinforced when Tophas falls asleep (67). Not only is the sleep itself an obvious similarity, but so also is the arrival of three pages who attempt to awaken Tophas, just as three messengers try to awaken Endimion. Finally, Tophas, after awakening, reveals a dream, just as does Endimion.

Having diverted the audience's attention with the antics of Sir Tophas, Lyly returns, in Act III, Scene iv, to the main thread of the story. With motifs adopted from folklore, this scene contrasts sharply with the preceding ones as it theorizes about love. There is here no Platonic ladder of love; rather, a dichotomy is created between love and friendship, with the latter clearly in the ascendancy. As a dramatic convention, friendship between men was never stronger than in the sixteenth century (friendship between women never seems to have had much force). One can, in fact, almost measure the development of English comedy by the degree to which conventions are sacrificed to reality.[20]

Until now Eumenides has played a very poor role as Endimion's confidant, but in Act III, Scene iv, he assumes a character and succumbs to the Endimion syndrome—he, too, falls in love with an unwilling female, and this parallelism once again imposes unity on the plot. The last part of the scene achieves additional structural unity through two devices: first, the notion of unity in variety introduced in Act I, Scene i, forms the basis of Geron's philosophy—"Is shee not alwaies *Cynthia,* yet seldome in the same bignesse; alwaies wauering in her waxing or wayning, that our bodies might the better bee gouerned, our seasons the daylier giue their increase; yet neuer to bee remooued from her course, as long as the heauens continue theirs? (174-178). Second, only Cynthia's kiss will release Endimion from the spell placed on him by Dipsas.

There is a natural division between the third and fourth acts. Eumenides has discovered the remedy, but he must be allowed time to return from his journey. Lyly thus repeats the pattern he employed in Act III—he focuses attention on Tellus (Scenes i and iii) and Sir Tophas (Scene ii). And as Lyly began with Tellus and Corsites in the third act, so he begins with them in the fourth. This time Tellus plays a silly trick on Corsites which accomplishes two ends: it further reveals Tellus's frivolous character; more importantly, it brings Tellus and Corsites back into the mainstream of the action. When Corsites, at Tellus's urging, tries to hide Endimion's body in a cave, two lines of action converge.

Act IV, Scene ii, begins by stressing the parallelism in the situation involving Endimion and Sir Tophas, and then exploits the comic potential in the similarity. But the scene degenerates toward the end into an irrelevant discussion about masterless men. With the appearance of the Master Constable and the Watch (line 73), all semblance of relevance disappears; the scene dissolves into a moment's fun, complete with a song.

In Act IV, Scene iii, Corsites joins Endimion and Tophas as sleeping lovers. His love for the whimsical Tellus has led him to violate Cynthia's command and as punishment the fairies have put him to sleep. At this point (IV.iii.42), Cynthia begins to distribute rewards and punishments. Semele is punished for her shrewishness, Corsites is forgiven for his offense, and Tellus is censured for her tricks. Cynthia thus displays her benevolence by dispensing justice combined with mercy.

By Act V, Scene i, the second major movement is almost completed. The curse on Endimion has been lifted, but his restoration is not complete—he has yet to regain his lost youth. Arising from the grave, as it were, Endimion explains his dream: "Me thought I sawe a Ladie passing faire, but verie mischeeuous; who in the one hande carried a knife with which shee offered to cut my throte, and in the other a looking-glasse, wherein seeing how ill anger became Ladies, shee refrained from intended violence" (81-85). The two ladies, anger and mercy, are followed by an old man who offers Endimion a book with three leaves containing counsels, policies, and pictures. Endimion twice refuses the book, and the old man twice tears a leaf in half. Finally, Endimion takes the book and the old man vanishes.

The crux of the dream lies, of course, in the last leaf; and Cynthia requests clarification of its significance, to which Endimion replies,

There portraid to life, with a colde quaking in euery ioynt, I behelde many wolues barking at thee *Cynthia*, who hauing ground their teeth to bite, did with striuing bleede themselues to death. There might I see ingratitude with an hundred eyes, gazing for benefites, and with a thousand teeth, gnawing on the bowelles wherein shee was bred. Trecherie stoode all cloathed in white . . . her handes bathed in blood. Enuye with a pale and megar face . . . stood shooting at starres. . . . There might I beholde Drones, or Beetles, . . . creeping vnder the winges of a princely Eagle, who

being carried into her nest, sought there to sucke that veine, that woulde
haue killed the Eagle. (119-132.)

Promising to tell Cynthia more later, Endimion concludes his explication involving the dangers that await a monarch.

Besides creating suspense by holding back the finale, Act V,
Scene ii, serves little purpose; moreover, the gulling of Sir Tophas
has, by now, become shopworn. As the final scene begins (V.iii),
Cynthia is again praised for her justice and mercy, qualities evident
in the second round of rewards and punishments she distributes.
After Tellus confesses her trickery and begs Cynthia's forgiveness,
the men and women are paired off: Endimion with Cynthia,
Eumenides with Semele, Corsites with Tellus, Geron with Dipsas,
and Tophas with Bagoa. The play thus ends with wedding bells, as
a good comedy should. It is doubtful, however, that the couples will
live happily ever after. In the Prologue, Lyly warned his audience
that *Endimion* was "neither Comedie nor Tragedie," a warning
that is realized in what should be the comic denouement. Lyly's
comic universe is too complicated and sophisticated to entertain un-
adulterated bliss.

Lyly captures the spirit of love in a net of skepticism. Celestial
love leads not to perfect union with the divine but to partial fulfillment, as Endimion's frustrated desire to possess Cynthia is
modulated into a graceful acceptance of his renewed youth. Romantic love finds its fulfillment in two tense alliances between roman-
tically inclined men and sharp-tongued females. The aged Geron is
reunited with Dipsas, but much too late; for love—and life—have
passed them by. Perhaps in the final analysis only the naturalistic—or biological—love of Sir Tophas achieves complete
fulfillment. He asks for little, and little is what he gets, but he
registers no complaints. After his fashion, he is no worse off than the
rest. Love may be the mysterious force of which poets sing, but its
lovely promise does not come true for the characters in *Endimion*.

III   Loves Metamorphosis (1588-1590)

As its title indicates, *Loves Metamorphosis* is about the strange
transformations effected by love. When Erisichthon, a woodsman,
fells a tree sacred to Ceres and inadvertently kills Fidelia, a nymph
who had metamorphosed herself in order to escape the advances of

a satyr, he is punished by Ceres, who sends Famine to destroy him. In order to feed the ravenous appetite which Famine creates, Erisichthon sells his daughter, Protea, to an unattractive merchant. Protea manages to escape, however, by supplicating the aid of Neptune, to whom she had sacrificed her virginity; Neptune transforms her into a fisherman and then into Ulysses, in which form she rescues her lover, Petulius, from a Siren. Meanwhile, Ceres's nymphs Nisa, Celia, and Niobe have rejected the advances of three foresters, thereby incurring the wrath of Cupid, who transforms them into a rock, a rose, and a bird. Cupid agrees to release them on the condition that Ceres will pardon Erisichthon. The nymphs ultimately regain their form, accept the foresters, and Erisichthon hosts the wedding feast.

Loves Metamorphosis is actually Lyly's last exploration in the romantic mode, for none of his last three plays is primarily concerned with love. *Midas* focuses on the craving for wealth and power, *The Woman in the Moon* is a satire on women, and *Mother Bombie* is a Roman comedy which sacrifices romance to intrigue. *Loves Metamorphosis* is not only the last of Lyly's romantic comedies but also his shortest comedy (1150 lines): it involves the fewest characters (fifteen); and, with the exception of *The Woman in the Moon*, it contains the fewest scenes (eleven). Perhaps because it is so short and direct, *Loves Metamorphosis* is Lyly's most exciting comedy. Event follows event in quick succession, as a threat hovers now over Erisichthon, now over Protea, now over Petulius, now over the nymphs of Ceres, until, finally, the darkness dissolves in the joyous sounds of the wedding feast. It is a straightforward comedy which hides nothing from audience or participants. Instead of exploiting dramatic irony, *Loves Metamorphosis* depends for interest on sensational incidents (such as nymph-slaughter), grotesque descriptions (such as that of Famine), shape-shifting, and other devices to prevent tediousness.

Although in many ways Lyly's simplest comedy, *Loves Metamorphosis* partakes of much of the formal regularity which characterized *Endimion*. A technique of repetition and alternation provides variety at the same time it ensures unity. Of the eleven scenes, five are devoted exclusively to the love interest involving the foresters and the nymphs of Ceres; four are devoted exclusively to concerns created by Erisichthon and his family (two scenes, I.ii and

V.iv, are shared by the two plot elements). Furthermore, the scenes are varied in such a way that the plot elements are consistently intermingled: never are two consecutive scenes devoted exclusively to one element.

The arrangement of the speaking parts also indicates this kind of regularity, for the characters are evenly divided in terms of the two major forces in the play. Cupid has his followers in Ramis, Montanus, Silvestris, Petulius and Protea; Ceres has her followers in Nisa, Celia, Niobe, Tirtena and Fidelia. Of the followers, the three foresters and the three nymphs are presented with all of the formality of a classical ballet. Each time the foresters appear, Ramis speaks first, followed by Montanus and Silvestris (so it is in I.i, III.i, IV.i, iii); only in the last scene does variation occur; in it, Ramis is followed by Silvestris rather than Montanus. The nymphs are similarly presented in a set order. Since Ramis loves Nisa, Montanus loves Celia, and Silvestris loves Niobe, the nymphs appear in this order when they are pursued by their lovers in Act III, Scene i. Elsewhere, they are less concerned with regularity, although Nisa always speaks first in the scenes which concern the love which the foresters show to them (I.ii, V.iv).

In no other Lylian play is love more central than in *Loves Metamorphosis*.[21] The play begins with it, is supported by it, and ends with it. Although Ceres is a powerful goddess, she must defer to Cupid because, as she admits herself, "Cupid was neuer conquered, and therefore must be flattered: Virginitie hath, and therefore must be humble" (II.i.43-45). This is not to say, however, that love's victory comes easy, for such is not the case. Petulius and Protea, the entirely human pair, achieve happiness only after overcoming the obstacles represented by Erisichthon, the Merchant, and the Siren. Here, again, Lyly returns to Roman comedy for his nubile lovers who are frustrated by an external obstacle, but in *Loves Metamorphosis* such lovers play a secondary role.

The greater part of the love interest is focused on the foresters and the nymphs of Ceres, who, like Petulius and Protea, hear wedding bells, but only after intense anguish and disillusionment. Joy does settle rather tenuously at the end of the play, but it must break through clouds of bitterness in order to spread its light. Nisa warns Ramis that he may find her frigid; Celia warns Montanus that she may, like the thorns on a rose, be the one to prick; and Niobe warns

Silvestris that she may cuckold him. Yet, in spite of the dire warnings, each Jack gets his Jill; and Cupid announces that "here is none but is happie" (V.iv. 166).

Actually, the play presents four, not three, nymphs of Ceres; but the boy actors of the Children of Paul's must have been breaking in a new actor, for Lyly assigns only two lines to Tirtena.[22] She is not paired with a lover; but she does balance the scales, for without her, Ceres would have only four followers to Cupid's five. Otherwise, her presence is entirely gratuitous.

In Act I, Scene i, the foresters carry on a Neoplatonic discussion about the power of love before they hang their verses on a tree. In Act I, Scene ii, the object of the verses are three nymphs of Ceres who obviously delight in the attention that they are receiving. The tone shifts abruptly, however, with the entrance of Erisichthon (I.ii. 58), a hardhearted woodsman who proceeds to chop down a tree in which is imprisoned Fidelia, a symbol of unfruitful chastity. Even though he realizes the enormity of his offense, Erisichthon is unrepentant, so the nymphs report the rape to Ceres, whose servant Fidelia had been. Ceres is, naturally, furious about the tree-cutting incident; and she sends for Famine, whom she describes in vivid detail:

> Thou canst not misse of her, if thou remember but her name; and that canst thou not forget, for that comming neere to the place, thou shalt find gnawing in thy stomacke. Shee lyeth gaping, and swalloweth nought but ayre; her face pale, and so leane, that as easily thou maiest through the verie skinne behold the bone, as in a glasse thy shadow; her haire long, blacke and shaggie; her eyes sunke so farre into her head, that shee looketh out of the nape of her necke; her lips white and rough; her teeth hollow and red with rustinesse; her skin so thin, that thou maiest as liuely make an Anatomie of her body, as shee were cut vp with Chirurgiõs; her maw like a drie bladder, her heart swolne bigge with wind, and all her bowels like Snakes working in her body. This monster when thou shalt behold, tell her my mind, and returne with speed. (II.i.16-28)

This passage, perhaps the finest descriptive one in all of Lyly's writings, is closely followed by a description of Cupid, who receives a visitation from Ceres and her nymphs, an action which symbolically represents the superiority of love over virginity: "He should bee a god blind and naked, with wings, with bowe, with

arrowes, with firebrands; swimming sometimes in the Sea, & playing sometimes on the shore; with many other deuices, which the
Painters, being the Poets Apes, haue taken as great paines to shad-
dow, as they to lie" (51-58). Here, however, the description does
not measure up to that of Famine. In fact, Lyly should not have
attempted a second description, for monsters generally evoke a
more sensuous response than angelic gods of love. However,
description is sometimes employed to good effect in *Loves
Metamorphosis;* and Lyly is always aware of the superior effect of
dramatic confrontations. In this scene, for example, he uses
stichomythia most effectively in discussing the nature and causes of
love (especially lines 87-117).

Act III, Scene i, consists of three parallel incidents that involve
the foresters, who chase their favorite nymphs across the stage,
complain about their aloofness, and try to entice them with the
delights of love. Together, the three incidents illustrate a subtle use
of incremental repetition. The first incident, the shortest, presents
Ramis in pursuit of Nisa, who hates love (I.i.25). But, although she
hates love, she is able to respond in a human fashion to love. The second incident, longer than the first but shorter than the third,
presents Montanus in pursuit of Celia, who mocks love (I.i.24). To
mock is to be less involved than to hate, thus Celia stands at one
remove from Nisa. The third, and last, incident, the longest of the
three, presents Silvestris in pursuit of Niobe, who thinks herself
above love (I.i.26). Of the three, Niobe is the least involved with
love, and thus she is the most dangerous threat to the spirit of
romance. It is she, in fact, who ultimately threatens her lover with
the greatest ignominy of all—she threatens to prove him a cuckold
(V.iv.150-152).

The foresters' unsuccessful amours culminate when, late in the
scene, they discover their love poems defaced with unflattering
appendices at the hands of the nymphs. They realize, too, that
Erisichthon's slaying of Fidelia has not made their quest any easier.
Unable to succeed in their pursuit of semi-divine maidens, the
foresters invoke the aid of Cupid, a divine patron. Meanwhile,
Erisichthon, now subject to the curse of Famine (III.ii), sells his
daughter, Protea, to a merchant in order to feed his insatiable
appetite. The merchant is a type of *leno,* or pimp, who owns the girl
in Roman comedy; and he must be overthrown by the clever ser-

vant so that his master will win the girl. There are no clever servants in *Loves Metamorphosis*, however, so Protea must turn to other sources of comfort. It is fitting, therefore, that she should, like the foresters before her, turn to divine aid, in this case to Neptune, to whom she had earlier sacrificed her maidenhood.

Although Lyly relegates the Protea-Petulius affair to the background in *Loves Metamorphosis*, he works very consciously and imaginatively with the situation. He assigns, for example, three blocking figures, instead of the usual one. Protea and Petulius are kept apart by (1) her father, (2) the merchant, and (3) the Siren (IV.ii). By eliminating the convenient figure of the clever servant, Lyly forces his characters to seek aid in more original ways. In this manner he is able to provide motivation for the appearance of Neptune, who would otherwise serve as a *deus ex machina*. Here, again, Lyly uses the old Classical formula in a fresh context.

Act IV, Scene i, is an obvious parallel to Act II, Scene i. Whereas in the earlier scene Ceres and her nymphs visited Cupid, now the three foresters do the same. After listening to their complaints, Cupid questions them about the nymphs. When he discovers that he has been mocked by the nymphs—something that Ceres told them never to do—he enlists the aid of the foresters in assigning their proper punishment. Together, Cupid and the foresters arrive at a form of punishment that will satisfy the demands of comic justice. Each of the nymphs will be punished according to her outstanding attribute: Ramis asks that Nisa, the coldhearted, be transformed into a stone; Montanus wants Celia, the beautiful, to become a flower so that she will realize that beauty is fleeting; and Silvestris asks that Niobe, the flighty, be transformed into a bird.[23]

Lyly returns to the Roman pattern in Act IV, Scene ii, which picks up the action where it left off in Act III, Scene ii, as Protea evades the merchant who has purchased her from her father. The pattern becomes more complex, however, when Protea desires to enjoy her lover, Petulius, who is endangered by a Siren. Protea, with the help of Neptune, who has already transformed her into a fisherman, disguises herself as Ulysses in order to save Petulius. However, *Loves Metamorphosis* departs from the Roman formula—and also from the technique employed in most of Lyly's comedies—in that it emphasizes the comic resolution. In *Campaspe*, Lyly handles the comic resolution rather hastily, as the happy union of Apelles and Campaspe is overshadowed by the Alexander story. In *Sapho*, there is no happy resolution, nor is there in *Endimion* (at least not in the "they lived happily ever after" sense). Only in *Gallathea* does Lyly provide a full comic resolution, but there it is implicit and reserved for a future moment outside the drama. (In this respect, it is significant that only *Gallathea, Endimion*, and *Loves Metamorphosis* have fifth acts that are appreciably longer than the other acts in the plays.) But in *Loves Metamorphosis* the action culminates in motifs of unification that distinguish the comedy from Lyly's other efforts, and these prefigure the resolutions of Shakespeare's "romantic" comedies.

In Act V, Scene i, for example, Ceres begs Cupid to release her nymphs. Cupid agrees, with the proviso that Ceres remove her spell on Erisichthon. After sundry penalties are meted out to offending parties, Ceres and Cupid part in friendship. This amiability, then, is the dominant tone for the rest of the last act. In Act V, Scene ii, Protea confesses to Petulius that her virginity had been claimed by Neptune, and he is quick to forgive.[24] Then they encounter the nymphs, still metamorphosed, who serve as an object lesson for all young lovers. Both Petulius and Protea vow never to violate the commandments of Cupid.

In Act V, Scene iii, the shepherds arrive preparatory to the grand finale. Silvestris and Ramis represent the extremes of the various attitudes toward love exhibited in *Loves Metamorphosis*. Silvestris is upset because his nymph will love him only under compulsion; he wants absolute love! Ramis, on the other hand, will settle for any kind of love at all. Reminiscent of Sir Tophas, Ramis says, "Let them [women] curse all day, so I may haue but one kisse at night" (19-20). By the final scene, the three nymphs of Ceres have been restored; and Erisichthon has been released from the curse of Famine. Because of his loyalty and forgiving nature, Petulius is rewarded with the lovely, although slightly used, Protea. But when the shepherds claim their mates, the nymphs announce that, rather than marry men, they would prefer to exist as stones, flowers, and birds. The gods thus intervene for the last time: when Cupid threatens to turn the nymphs into monsters if they refuse love, Ceres begs them to reconsider. Finally, after registering their complaints with the suitors for having had them transformed in the first place, the nymphs agree to marry the men.

Loves Metamorphosis marks two variations in Lyly's usual techniques. First, he gives the comic denouement a rich form. Even though the three nymphs are reluctant to the last, their final acquiescence appears to spring from a natural desire for sexual fulfillment. Thus, the erotic impulse in this play is not frustrated as in *Sapho*, subordinated as in *Campaspe*, or mitigated as in *Endimion;* indeed, only the ending of *Gallathea* approximates that of *Loves Metamorphosis*. Second, *Loves Metamorphosis* is the only Lyly comedy that lacks witty servants, or their equivalents. As a result of both of these departures, *Loves Metamorphosis* is one of the most universal of Lyly's plays and one likely to appeal to an audience vague about the details of Elizabethan social history. Footnote humor is seldom humorous; and the procession of Roman characters named Granicus, Manes, Cryticus, Molus, Dares, and Samias does not endear Lyly to contemporary audiences. When Lyly bypasses them in favor of native English rustics, as he does in *Gallathea*, one is struck by the freshness of a Rafe, Robin and Peter. But most of all, one is struck by the form of *Loves Metamorphosis*, for it is through form that comedy impresses one most. Perhaps what is ultimately the most basic form of comedy, an erotic intrigue leading to sexual fulfillment, is the most successful. *Loves Metamorphosis* suggests that it is.[25]

CHAPTER 5

Late Plays

I   Midas (*January 6, 1589/90*)

M IDAS, Lyly's least successful play, lacks the exciting action of *Loves Metamorphosis*, the psychological depth of *Endimion*, and the controlled unity of *Campaspe*. Lyly's own description of *Midas* remains the best: "Time hath confounded our mindes, our mindes the matter; but all commeth to this passe, that what heretofore hath beene serued in seuerall dishes for a feaste, is now minced in a charger for a Gallimaufrey" (Prologue, 16-19).

Midas is a straightforward comedy which does not exploit dramatic irony. Unfortunately, however, the story of the Midas touch, at least as handled by Lyly, lacks sophistication. The narrative is so bare, in fact, that Lyly feels compelled to dress it with the story of Midas and the ass's ears. One would think that the curse of the Midas touch would be sufficient to inculcate prudence in Midas, but in Lyly's play, it is not enough. When Midas is released from the golden curse, he is as foolish as he was at the start—thus, the ass's ears! Lyly does, however, achieve variety because the first incident is dependent upon Midas's desire for worldly prosperity and the second upon Midas's inferior esthetic taste. Midas, in short, chooses unwisely, both in matters that pertain to the flesh and to the spirit.

The play begins with Midas faced with a choice: Bacchus, in return for Midas's hospitality, has offered him whatever his heart desires. Midas's three counselors, Eristus, Martius, and Mellacrites, proffer advice. Eristus tells him to ask for a woman; Martius, for worldly domination; Mellacrites, for wealth. Midas, who follows the advice of Mellacrites, asks that everything he touch be turned to gold. He soon learns his mistake and begs to be relieved of the touch, which is effected when he washes in the waters of the river Pactolus.

At this point, a second movement begins where Midas serves as judge in a musical competition between Apollo and Pan. With Midas's unfailing flair for inferiority, he declares Pan the winner. Apollo's punishment takes the form of ass's ears which Midas tries to conceal beneath a crown. But his punishment has been bruited about by nymphs and shepherds, and echoed by the reeds in the field. Midas finally presents himself before Apollo's oracle at Delphi, where the curse is removed. Midas returns to Phrygia determined to rule sensibly and to halt his unsuccessful war against Lesbos.

The fabric of the play is actually composed of four threads. First, sections deal with Midas's touch and ears; second, a very tenuous love interest involves Eristus and Caelia, the daughter of Mellacrites (almost exclusively contained in the second act); third, Midas's daughter Sophronia renders diatribes against love (see II.i and III.iii); fourth, the low characters, the pages and Motto the barber, provide some slapstick humor (they appear once in each act). The sections involving Midas and the pages illustrate the moral that to aspire beyond one's limitations is to invite disaster, and thereby ensures for *Midas* a universality that takes it well beyond Lyly's own time and place.

Actually, *Midas* is an illustration of the loose methods of construction that characterize Elizabethan comedy. Although Lyly usually subscribed to Classical notions of exclusivity and compression, he was nevertheless a product of his own time; and his era was not averse to mingling two or sometimes three and four stories in a single play. Pitted against the Classical compactness of *Ralph Roister Doister* is the native English emphasis on variety represented by Greene's *Friar Bacon and Friar Bungay*, to which *Midas* is closely allied. Lyly is writing a comedy, not an epic; and one should not be surprised that he employs two stories traditionally associated with Midas.

The problem with *Midas* is not that it has two stories, or that it is political propaganda, or that it stresses debate at the expense of passion.[1] The problem is rather that the characters are insuf-

ficiently motivated. Midas, for example, receives from Bacchus a
single wish, whereupon he immediately consults with his advisers.
Eristus advises Midas to seek a mistress; Martius, to seek world
domination. The alternatives are clear: Midas can make either love
or war. But, Mellacrites, the third adviser, has a suggestion that
enables Midas to make love *and* war. In a speech reminiscent of
Volpone, Mellacrites urges Midas to seek wealth which will insure
both sex and power.

Is it not gold that maketh the chastest to yeeld to lust, the honestest to
lewdnes, the wisest to follie, the faithfullest to deceit, and the most holy in
heart, to be most hollow of hart? In this word Gold are all the powers of the
gods, the desires of men, the woonders of the worlde, the miracles of
nature, the losenes of fortune and triumphs of time. By gold may you shake
the courts of other Princes, and haue your own setled; one spade of gold
vndermines faster than an hundred mattocks of steele. Would one be
thought religious & deuout? *Quantum quisque sua nummorum seruat in
arca, tantum habet & fidei:* Religions ballance are golden bags. Desire you
vertue? *quaerenda pecunia primum est, virtus post nummos:* the first staire
of vertue is money. Doeth anie thirst after gentrie, and wish to be esteemed
beautiful? & *genus & formam regina pecunia donat:* king Coin hath a mint
to stamp gentlemen, and art to make amiablenes. I denie not but loue is
sweet, and the marrowe of a mans minde, that to conquere kings is the
quintessence of the thoughts of kings: why then follow both, *Aurea sunt
vere nunc saecula, plurimus auro venit honos, auro conciliatur amor:* it is a
world for gold; honor and loue are both taken vp on interest. (I.i.40-59)

Although the speech is a good one, the problem of motivation still
remains unsolved. Midas, motivated by the double promise of sex
and power contained in Mellacrites's speech, chooses gold.
However, the sex promise is manufactured for the sake of the decision; for Midas never again refers to it. Midas is not looking for a
girl; he is looking for power. But if he had chosen power as Martius
advised, there would have been no play.

An abrupt change in tone is signaled by the appearance of the
witty pages in Act I, Scene ii, who begin, in a slightly salacious
manner, by debating the charms of Elizabethan fashions in general
and of Mellacrites's daughter (Caelia) in particular; and when
Pipenetta, Caelia's maid, enters, the pages turn their wit against
her. A new complication is introduced in Act II, Scene i, when

Eristus, Midas's counselor, announces his love for Caelia. That his love is real and earnest can be deduced from the symptoms he displays:

Ah, *Caelia,* if kinges saye they loue and yet dissemble, who dare say that they dissemble, and not loue? They commaunde the affections of others yeeld, and their owne to be beleeued. My teares which haue made furrowes in my cheekes, and in mine eyes fountaines: my sighes, which haue made of my heart a furnace, and kindled in my head flames: my body that melteth by peecemeale, and my mind that pineth at an instant, may witnesse that my loue is both vnspotted, & vnspeakeable, *Quorum si singula duram flectere non poterant, deberent omnia mentem.* (27-35)

Eristus is the play's spokesman for love, just as Martius is for war. Interestingly enough, Sophronia wants nothing to do with either of them or, for that matter, with Mellacrites. She advises Midas, her father, to visit the temple of Bacchus and to beg that his gift be withdrawn.

In the first act, Lyly juxtaposes the first two scenes; he repeats the juxtaposition in the second act as the entrance of the witty pages in Act II, Scene ii, sharply contrasts with the serious tone of Act II, Scene i. This time, instead of toying with Pipenetta, Licio and Petulus, the pages toy with the notion of the cosmic egg.[2] Structurally, the second act repeats the first: in each, a scene of Courtly seriousness is followed by a scene of frivolity. This arrangement of scenes is repeated in the third act, as the first scene is again devoted to the Courtly group; the second, to the pages. This time, however, a third scene adds variety.

Act III, Scene i, is the least dramatic scene in the entire play. Out of a total of eighty-nine lines, seventy-four are devoted to a speech by Midas in which he laments his unfortunate situation. Taken out of context, the speech offers an interesting contrast with many of the martial sentiments expressed in the first of Lyly's comedies, *Alexander and Campaspe.* And, as such, the speech again illustrates the amazing complexity of Lyly's world view, one in which nothing should be taken for granted. Alexander, for example, received praise for his decision to make war, not love. With Midas it is quite a different matter.

The action picks up again in Act III, Scene ii, as Motto, the royal

barber, comes to recover Midas's golden beard, which has been
conned from him by Licio and Petulus. Arrangements are made for the
return of the beard, but only on the condition that Motto ease a
toothache which is afflicting Petulus. Act III, Scene iii, is reminiscent of Renaissance courtesy books, such as Castiglione's *The
Courtier*, not to mention Lyly's own *Euphues* and *Euphues and His
England*. In an effort to while away an idle evening, Sophronia and
her friends decide to tell stories about love. Unlike similar situations
in the courtesy books, however, the group in *Midas* is composed entirely of females; therefore, none of the male-female debate which
enlivens *Euphues and His England* is present.

The first scene of Act IV is again devoted to the royal problems,
here prefaced by the confrontation between Pan and Apollo, who
are about to engage in a recital contest. Asked by the gods to judge
the contest, Midas gets involved in another sensitive situation. Even
though the nymphs vote for Apollo, Midas, with characteristic ob-
tuseness, votes for Pan. In fact, there is little to choose between the
songs; about the most that can be said for them is that they rhyme.
The fact that both songs are equally inferior indicates that what
Midas is actually voting for is the singer, not the song. His selection
of Pan in preference to Apollo thus suggests Midas's warped
hierarchy of values; for, given the opportunity, Midas invariably
makes the wrong choice. This time his reward for folly is a pair of
ass's ears: he has acted like an ass; now he looks like one as well.
Like Bottom in *A Midsummer Night's Dream*, Midas has made an
ass of himself.

In Act IV, Lyly substitutes shepherds for the pages one has come
to expect in the second scene, reserving them for the third scene. In
discussing Midas's ears, the shepherds attribute to him additional
animal characteristics. The resulting montage is of a highly
ridiculous Machiavellian tyrant: "I say he is no Lion, but a monster;
peec'd with the craftines of the fox, the crueltie of the tyger, the
rauening of the woolfe, the dissembling of the Hyena, he is worthy
also to haue the eares of an asse" (27-30).

In Act IV, Scene iii, the witty pages turn their arrows against a
huntsman, thereby providing a moment of fun at the expense of
unity. A case might be made that as the huntsman aspires toward
royal prerogatives, he represents the kind of mentality which
characterizes Midas. The huntsman's overthrow at the hands of

Licio and Petulus repeats, then, the overthrow of Midas at the hands of Apollo. Whatever possible interpretations might be placed upon the scene, one thing is certain—the scene dissolves into a low-comic encounter fraught with sexual innuendo.[3]

Act IV, Scene iv, is primarily expository, as the rest of the royal party learns Midas's secret, which he has kept hidden under his crown. Concerned for his welfare, Midas's counselors seek him out. When they are joined by Sophronia and her ladies-in-waiting, the reeds whisper to them all that "*Mydas* the King hath asses eares" (53-54).

The last act is structured in the same way as the first four acts: the first scene is devoted to the royal characters; the second, to the pages. Furthermore, themes with which the play began are now repeated at the end. Sex, power, and wealth, symbolized by the three choices open to Midas in Act I, Scene i, now are repeated as Midas himself offers two options to anyone who can "tell the reason of these reedes creaking" (49-50): his daughter (sex), or a dukedom (power and wealth). Finally, as in the story about the Emperor's new clothes, Midas threatens to execute anyone who refers to his ass's ears.

In Act V, Scene ii, Licio and Petulus, having been duped by Motto, plot their revenge. When Pipenetta brings news of Midas's proclamation, Licio and Petulus immediately envision themselves as winning the prize. Here the pages step outside their normal roles as witty servants and become presumptuous asses by aspiring beyond their station. Their aspirations are short-lived, however, for the moment that Motto enters, Lucio and Petulus forget their grand designs and turn on Motto instead. In their plot to encourage Motto to say that Midas has ass's ears, the pages return to their roles as gullers. When they succeed in trapping Motto into a public statement exposing Midas's ass's ears, Lucio and Petulus exact in exchange for their silence the golden beard which Motto had earlier conned from them. Licio and Petulus disappear at this point in the play; their own pretensions are not exploited by Lyly.

The final scene (V.iii) is devoted entirely to Midas. No mention is made of the servants, or of the Eristus-Caelia story, or of the Sophronia anti-love theme. The latter two elements were introduced in Act II, but the Eristus-Caelia story is mentioned only in Act II, Scene i, and Act II, Scene ii, and left unresolved; Sophronia's anti-romantic bias appears again in Act III, Scene iii, but is not fully resolved. The fact that she tells her father that she will marry if he desires (V.i) suggests a resolution of sorts, but it is not reached dramatically. Finally, Midas offers sacrifices, is forgiven by Apollo, loses his ass's ears, and promises to become a model ruler.

Structurally, *Midas* is at the same time one of Lyly's tightest and loosest plays. There is strict regularity in the manner in which the scenes are distributed: the first scene in every act is devoted, in part at least, to Midas; the second to the pages, except in the fourth act where the first two scenes are devoted to Midas and the third to the pages. Yet Midas and the pages never meet. There is nothing unusual about this fact, but the result is that much of the potential dramatic force is lost. One cannot imagine *Lear* without the encounters between Lear and the Fool.

The minor themes in *Midas* are left undeveloped. Eristus is pictured as the prostrate lover and Caelia as the coy lady from the Petrarchan tradition, yet after Act II, Scene ii, their intrigue is ignored. Similarly, in Act II, Scene i, Sophronia is established as a man-hater, a pallid sixteenth-century Woman's Liberation advocate; but, after one additional reference to this theme (III.iii), it too is ignored. Perhaps the casual handling of these themes, not the double Midas story, led Lyly to write, "If wee present a minglemangle, our fault is to be excused, because the whole worlde is become an Hodge-podge" (Prologue, 19-20).

Midas has occasioned little critical enthusiasm, although J. Dover Wilson includes Pipenetta among Lyly's more effective characterizations.[4] Perhaps the most rewarding way to approach *Midas* is to examine its moral implications, not its political allegory, for in doing so its universality, not its topicality, emerges.[5]

II   The Woman in the Moon (*1591-1595*)

The Woman in the Moon, like *Midas*, turns on irony of situation, as outcome again proves contrary to expectation. The plot of *The Woman in the Moon* involves four lonely shepherds, at whose request Nature creates a woman, Pandora (why she does not create four women is uncertain), whom she endows with the attributes usually associated with the seven planets: Saturn's "deep conceit," Jupiter's "high thoughts," and the like. The Planets, angry that they were not consulted, plot Pandora's downfall. Saturn endows her with moodiness; Jupiter, with ambition and disdain; Mars, with warlike vigor. Variety is introduced in the person of Sol, the virtuous planet, who implants in Pandora gentleness, kindness, love, liberality, chastity, mercy, and provides her with the gifts of poetry and prophecy as characteristic of womankind.

Venus is upset, however, at the sight of a sober, virtuous Pandora; she prefers a witty, amorous, and wanton creature. Under Venus's influence, Pandora loves all of the shepherds. Mercury then sees to it that Pandora's indiscretions are revealed to her lover, Stesias; and Mercury also endows her with gifts of treachery and deception. When Stesias is finally convinced that the stories of Pandora's unfaithfulness must be true, she deceives him into doubting his own conviction. She thereupon arranges a meeting between Stesias and the other shepherds at which her innocence will be declared. After soothing Stesias's ruffled feathers, Pandora repeats her deception on the other three shepherds, so that each believes he has been singled out for special attention. As the shepherds pine for Pandora, she and her beloved clown, Gunophilus, carry on a grotesque parody of the language of love:

PAN.   When I forsake thee, then heauen it selfe shal fall.
GUN.   No, God forbid, then perhaps we should haue Larkes. (IV.i.290-91)

Finally, Luna assumes control of Pandora, whereupon she is characterized by fickleness, sloth, folly and madness. When one encounters Pandora and Gunophilus again, they are almost at the seacoast, but Pandora suddenly grows angry and refuses to travel farther. Stesias discovers them and persuades Pandora to return to his bower. But, after she falls asleep, the other shepherds convince Stesias of her infidelity. Even though the Planets speak in her defense, Stesias will have no more of Pandora. Since she is no longer desired by mortals, Pandora is given refuge in one of the Planet's orbits. Each Planet desires her, but Pandora selects Luna because the attributes which please her most are fickleness, frenzy, and forgetfulness.

Because Stesias rejected Pandora, he is sentenced by Nature to follow Pandora in the Moon. Then, in an inverted Orpheus-Euridice relationship, Stesias tears off a branch of hawthorn bush and threatens to scratch Pandora's face if she ever turns around to

look at him. Finally, Nature orders Pandora to make the Moon inconstant; it is to reign at women's nuptials and births, and it is to
make women mutable, fantastical, childish, foolish in their desires
and, when they cannot have their will, stark mad.

The Woman in the Moon allows the audience to participate in an
experience determined by the gods. In this play, Lyly splits the
human and divine characters in such a way that the audience ends
up with the gods. From the moment that the Planets decide to
punish Pandora, the play is dependent upon knowledge that is
possessed by the gods and the audience but not by Pandora and the
other humans. It is essential, of course, that the audience share in
the divine knowledge; for if it did not know that Pandora's conduct
was influenced by the gods, her role would be incomprehensible.
Instead of a study in inconstancy, Pandora would be a study in
irrationality, quite a different thing; and Lyly wants to portray a
fickle woman, not a mad one. From a twentieth-century point of
view, The Woman in the Moon is Lyly's most universal comedy.
Few explanatory notes are required for the modern reader because
there is little topical humor. As a result, there are no obstacles
between the reader and the text, and the action moves forward in a
manner that is at once crisp and clear.

The Woman in the Moon is the only play of Lyly's which omits
the name of Paul's boys from the title page, thus suggesting a
production date subsequent to 1591, the year that the Paul's boys
suffered their inhibition. If the play was produced as late as 1594-
1595, it is possible that Lyly picked up a few hints from
Shakespeare's A Midsummer Night's Dream. The two plays share
important similarities: under the spell of Luna, Pandora falls in love
with a clown, Gunophilus; under the spell of a magic flower,
Titania falls in love with a clown, Bottom. Since the dating is uncertain, the direction of the influence remains unclear.

The fact that The Woman in the Moon is in blank verse, the only
one of Lyly's plays that is, also suggests a late date of composition,
but not one so late as 1595. Although the verse is more supple than
that of The Arraignment of Paris and The Misfortunes of Arthur,
plays to which Bond compares The Woman in the Moon to Lyly's
advantage,[6] it is not so pliable as the blank verse that held the
English stage by 1595. Practically every line in The Woman in the
Moon is end-stopped, and Lyly betrays a predilection for beginning

lines with the same sounds, perhaps a verse manifestation of his
Euphuistic urges, a device harking back to pre-Marlovian blank
verse. Characteristic of Lyly's verse techniques are the following:
Beginning lines with identical sounds:

> Thou are indowd with *Saturns* deep conceit,
> Thy minde as hawte as *Iupiters* high thoughts,
> Thy stomack Lion-like, like *Mauors* hart,
> Thine eyes bright beamde, like *Sol* in his array,
> Thy cheekes more fayre, then are faire *Venus* cheekes,
> Thy tongue more eloquent then *Mercuries*,
> Thy forehead whiter then the siluer Moones:
> Thus haue I robd the Planets for thy sake. (I.i.95-102)

Beginning alternate lines with identical words, or sounds:

> And these my lippes that did blaspheme thy loue,
> Shall speake thee fayre and blesse thee with a kisse;
> And this my hand that hurt thy tender side,
> Shall first with herbes recure the wound it made, (III.i.18-21)

These, and similar devices, are found more often in earlier English
blank verse; and they argue for a date of composition closer to the
beginning of the last decade of the sixteenth century. They suggest
also that whatever influence may be at work began with Lyly rather
than with Shakespeare. Indeed, whatever the defects in versi-
fication, *The Woman in the Moon* reveals an originality that is
characteristic of Lyly.[7] The notion of planetary influence was vital
in Lyly's time; but, as T. W. Baldwin points out, the idea of using
that importance dramatically was not common.[8] *The Rare
Triumphs of Love and Fortune*, which Bond cites as Lyly's model,[9]
presents contending goddesses, but they are not put in the form of
Planets.

    Although Baldwin sees *The Woman in the Moon* as continuing in
a tradition of conflicting powers which began in *Campaspe* with
abstract emotions, it is actually moving in quite a different direction. In *Sapho*, the abstractions were personified as Venus entered
the conflict; in *Gallathea*, two personifications, chastity and love,
battle in the persons of Diana and Venus; in *Loves Metamorphosis*,
Ceres and Cupid are combatants; in *Midas*, the struggle again

returns to the conflicting abstractions of *Campaspe*. In all of these plays, however, the conflict is localized in two or three principals. But in *The Woman in the Moon* the conflict rages between Pandora and seven divinities, four shepherds and one clown.

Bernard Huppé is on the right track when he argues that Lyly is attempting in *The Woman in the Moon* to create woman incarnate, and that each of her psychological traits is represented by one of the divinities.[10] In this sense, then, the play will admit of no resolution, at least not in the sense that *Campaspe* is resolved. There can be no resolution because there is really no conflict. What passes for conflict is merely complexity, the inner confusion and turmoil characteristic of Lyly's view of women. What Lyly presents, then, is an Elizabethan "Portrait of a Lady" done in the allegorical mode and framed in satire.

G. K. Hunter denies that *The Woman in the Moon* is a satire on women. By way of evidence he cites the *topoi* that were available to Lyly from Medieval and Renaissance tradition, and Lyly's avoidance of them. He also cites the pastoral quality of the play, arguing that "it can hardly be pastorally poetic and pageant-like in showing the actions of the gods, and yet remain satiric." Finally, Hunter claims that "satire invites us to make a judgment, and this is no part of the appeal of *The Woman in the Moon*."[11] In spite of Hunter's objections, a case for satire can be made. First, it is not true that Lyly avoids those *topoi* that had become associated with satire of women—love of finery, concealment of ugliness, vanity, pretentiousness, sensuality, and false modesty. Under the influence of Jupiter (II), Pandora's melancholy disposition leads to self-pride (the *topoi* of vanity and pretentiousness); under the influence of Venus (III), she becomes wanton (the *topus* of sensuality); under the influence of Mercury (IV), she learns to deceive (the *topus* of false modesty). It is true that she evinces no love of finery; neither does she conceal ugliness. The latter may be explained by the fact that the role was played by a young boy.

Hunter's second point, that *The Woman in the Moon* is pastorally poetic and therefore non-satiric, is curious since *As You Like It* is pastorally poetic and satiric at the same time. Both plays, however, are lightly satiric; they are neither heavy with irony nor dripping with sarcasm; but a writer does not have to beat with a cudgel in order to make his point. Hunter's last point, that satire invites one to make a judgment and that *The Woman in the Moon* does not, is too simplistic a judgment. It is highly questionable, for example, that Jonathan Swift's *Gulliver's Travels* or George Orwell's *Animal Farm* invite one to make a judgment; it would be truer to say that they determine one's judgment. After all, what are the alternatives? To sanction the position of either the Emperor of Lilliput or the chief pig is to proclaim idiocy or moral corruption.

Actually, as Michael R. Best claims, Pandora is not so much a character as an anticipation of Ben Jonson's "humours" types. Lyly's play is basically static, composed as it is of a series of tableaux which illustrate or epitomize various "humours" imposed by the rule of the gods.[12] Thematically, the play is closely allied with *Loves Metamorphosis*, but from an antithetical point of view: in this play, human imperfection is accepted and resolved by the action of love; in *The Woman in the Moon*, imperfection is rejected with the result that immortality is achieved at the expense of happiness.

Peter Saccio argues that Pandora becomes a personality before one's very eyes. When one first encounters her, she is a blank, possessing only physical attributes and mental and emotional potentiality. She has no personality, however, until the gods get to work. Saccio's case is weak, however, for he makes no effort to demonstrate that Pandora's so-called personality is a result of her decisive choice or action rather than something merely imposed on her from without. The fact that her emotional states "naturally slide one into the next"[13] is no proof, for all emotional states slide "one into the next." Emotions are continuous, not discrete. Although Saccio credits *The Woman in the Moon* with more subtlety than it actually possesses, he is correct in arguing that Pandora's final decision is based on more than mere capriciousness. Since she has moved quickly in the play from one emotional state to another, she has no real alternative to selecting Luna's sphere for her permanent home. Change has been the manner of her existence on earth; now it provides her permanent home in Heaven.

The Woman in the Moon is Lyly's most cerebral comedy in that it tends toward abstraction more than the others do. Of the twenty characters, all but six are abstractions. Even though they are given human form, they are far too simplistic to approximate men and women; they are without complexity in either action or motivation. Nature, Concord, and Discord are a trinity of contending powers that initially motivates the comedy; and Nature alone ultimately concludes it. Within this framework, the other deities, as well as the human characters, operate.

The intellectual nature of *The Woman in the Moon* is established in the opening scene as Nature, surveying her handiwork in Utopia, registers her satisfaction at everything she sees except the frown on Discord's face. The frown is present because, no matter how mightily she labors to introduce contraries, Concord unites the contending forces. Nature then offers an explanation which foreshadows the Hegalian dialectic:

> I tell thee *Discord* while you twaine attend
> On *Natures* traine, your worke must prooue but one;
> And in your selues though you be different,
> Yet in my seruice must you well agree.
> For *Nature* workes her will from contraries,—(I.i.25-29)

Although *The Woman in the Moon*, perhaps because it is in verse, contains little of what is generally considered Euphuism, there is in Nature's opening speeches an attitude expressed which reflects Lyly's world view. The essence of his thought, whether in the plays or in the prose narratives, lies in opposition, especially in antitheses which assume the form of paradoxes. In Lyly's works, "things seems [sic] to engender their contraries rather than their likenesses. . . . Nothing is uniformly of one property. Everything contains within it the seeds of self-contradiction: . . . The more absolute of its kind a thing may appear to be, the more certain it is that somewhere within it lies its own antithesis, its anti-self. . . . Whereas his predecessors had aimed at exposing a hidden consistency in the workings of nature, Lyly ranged the affinities and the antipathies side by side so as to unveil the contradictions in nature, the infinite inconsistency of the world."[14] The infinite inconsistency of the world of *The Woman in the Moon* is represented by the conflicting forces of Concord and Discord, the two handmaidens of Nature. And, even though the play concludes with an apotheosis, usually a sign of divine harmony, Discord is far from overcome. As Michael Best points out,

> We might expect a happy ending. However, . . . Stesias refuses to be

reconciled to Pandora. The gods, and later Nature, descend from their machines but are unable to manipulate a happy ending. To make amends for the interference of the gods, Nature places Pandora on their level—in Luna's sphere, after some envious competition amongst the gods for the privilege. Stesias continues to reject Pandora, though he cannot now kill her. His passion . . . has become transcendent, and . . . he is immortalized in hate as Pandora's attendant. He plucks the hawthorn bush which Gunophilus had been changed into, intent still on revenge. . . . This act of defiance, in which Stesias refuses to accept the imperfection of Pandora's love, is the one action which the gods could not control; Stesias asserts his independence at the expense of a bitter immortality. He is perpetuated as the paradoxical figure of the jealous lover, hating in proportion to the depth of his original love, a kind of reverse to the image of the lovers seen by Keats on the Grecian urn. The conclusion of the play is a static tableau of Discord.[15]

The entire universe of *The Woman in the Moon* thus gives testimony to Lyly's peculiar vision of paradox and instability. In this sense, then, the comedy is Euphuistic even though the rhetorical devices usually associated with Euphuism are definitely played in a minor key.

The "Portrait of a Lady" which Lyly presents in *The Woman in the Moon* is one which has appeared to a greater or lesser extent throughout his works. Lucilla in *Euphues*, Lais in *Campaspe*, the Queen and her ladies in *Sapho and Phao*, Tellus in *Endimion*, the nymphs of Ceres in *Loves Metamorphosis*, and Sophronia in *Midas* are all versions of the portrait. As the English dramatist who brought to the stage the sixteenth-century attitudes toward love, in all their variety and complexity, Lyly could never ascribe wholeheartedly to the notion of romantic love. Always a certain reticence, if not outright rejection, is apparent whenever Lyly writes about the subject. Wedding bells and marriage feasts, traditional in English comedy, are not endemic in Lyly's plays, especially in the later ones. Although *Campaspe* and *Gallathea* end with wedding bells, *Sapho and Phao* does not. *Endimion* ends with marriages in the offing, but not for the protagonist; and one questions whether the lesser characters will "live happily ever after." *Loves Metamorphosis* ends with wedding bells, but the heroine is slightly soiled, hardly the virgin of romance tradition. *Midas* has little to do with love, and *The Woman in the Moon* ends on an anti-romantic note. Finally, in *Mother Bombie*, probably his last play, Lyly turns to Italianate intrigue comedy.

Along with *Mother Bombie*, *The Woman in the Moon* is Lyly's most unusual comedy; and it is perhaps his best. Even though the verse is wooden, the simplicity of action and clarity of characterization work together to produce a universal English comedy. The witty pages are gone, the Euphuistic devices are missing, but their loss is balanced by freshness and vigor. The wit of the pages was rooted in sixteenth-century social customs, the Euphuistic devices in sixteenth-century rhetorical tradition—neither is in favor today. In their place, one has a wit that transcends time and a Euphuism that is embedded in the very fabric of thought.

III   Mother Bombie (*1590's*)

If the dating is accurate, Lyly's simplest and most complex comedies were written at about the same time in his career. *The Woman in the Moon* represents the straightforward Lyly; *Mother Bombie*, the intricate Lyly. He is intricate, but not necessarily profound; for the analysis of love in *Mother Bombie* is superficial compared with that in *Endimion*. The superficiality can be accounted for in part by the fact that *Mother Bombie* is an intrigue comedy which emphasizes plot at the expense of theme and characterization. Like all intrigue comedies, *Mother Bombie* ruthlessly exploits dramatic irony. The authority figures in the play are seldom in possession of the whole truth, but the audience usually knows exactly what is happening. The pages manage to outwit the fathers because of the latter's natural stupidity combined with inadequate sources of information. The audience, sharing in the information possessed by the pages, is thus able to sympathize with the lovers and to delight at the inevitable overthrow of the fathers.

T. W. Baldwin's summary of *Mother Bombie* communicates the light tone and suggests the geometrical structure of the play:

There are four fathers, each with a child whom he wishes to get married, and each with a comic servant. Two boys and two girls should equal one double wedding. Two of the fathers wish to have their children marry; but each knows that his own child is an idiot and wishes to conceal the fact from the other parent until after the match. The children of the other two parents wish to marry each other, but their parents object. Each of these

parents wishes to have his child marry one of the idiot children. The story
thus begins with everything at odds, and the problem is to put it at evens.
Since Lyly did not wish to be so realistic as to have two idiots marry, he
provided a third couple to be substituted for them at the crucial moment, so
that the double wedding might occur. As usual in Lyly, this couple simply
wanders through the play until it is needed in the fifth act, without any
previous hint of any business it may have there. A woman is required to
mother the two idiots, substitute them for wise children, and appear in the
fifth act to set all straight. A wise woman, Mother Bombie, . . . is a wholly
superfluous piece of atmosphere so far as the necessary plot machinery is
concerned. She merely tells riddling fortunes to each seeker after
knowledge, her only real contribution being to advise the mother of the
cradle-changed idiots to confess the substitution, and even at that the advice was not needed.
    . . . The natural point of attack is to get the primary sane couple
married. This will remove their objecting parents as disturbing influences
from the idiot couple, whose parents can then agree that they shall be
married. The solution is brought about by the four comic servants, who plot
to get the sane couple married. This marriage removes the disturbing influence for the idiot couple. . . . All that then remains is to substitute the
second sane couple for the idiots and have another wedding. . . . It is all
very simple geometry, with one algebraic substitution.[16]

   According to G. K. Hunter, *Mother Bombie* is not a comedy of
situation. The characters are not caught up in their past errors nor
are their follies revealed, as they would be in a Terentian comedy. It
is, rather, a play of wit in which the pages, placed at the center of
the action, outwit everyone else. Hunter thus includes *Mother Bombie* in the group of plays unified through subplot intrigue. Wit con-
trols the play; wit unifies the play; and, where wit receives so much
emphasis and where characters are so much in control of themselves, wit lends an air of mystery and misunderstanding to the
play.[17]
   Hunter is undoubtedly correct in arguing that wit dominates the
play, but he is incorrect in claiming that *Mother Bombie* is not a
comedy of situation in the Terentian manner. The wit, in fact, arises
out of situation and is, therefore, dependent upon situation. Love is
the principle theme, and erotic impulse moves the action. Interfering fathers threaten the formation of a new, healthier society
based on mutual love and compassion. The fathers in *Mother Bombie*
are, of course, the authority figures; and, as such, they are an in-

dication of the corruption which has infected healthy impulses in society. They are overthrown in much the same way that Ralph Roister Doister and Sir Tophas are overthrown by witty pages; but, were it not for the traditional comic situation of crusty fathers attempting to frustrate their children's erotic desires, there would be no vehicle for the wit of the pages. The wit, in short, is generated by situation.

The first act of *Mother Bombie* presents three scenes similar in form and content; in each, a father attempts to dispose of a child in marriage. The first two scenes are virtually identical: in Act I, Scene i, Memphio enlists the support of his servant, Dromio, to marry his idiot son, Accius, to Silena, the daughter of a rich farmer, Stellio. Dromio, whose name is indicative of his literary heritage, is a typical Roman witty page who promises to help; but, in reality, he plans to gull his master. In Act I, Scene ii, Stellio enlists the support of his servant, Riscio, to marry his idiot daughter, Silena, to Accius, son to Memphio. Riscio promises to help, but he plans in reality to work with Dromio in order to gull the two old fathers.

The implications of the first two scenes are developed in the third, in which a new set of lovers, Candius and Livia, are introduced along with their fathers, Sperantus and Prisius. The fathers object, naturally, to the mutual affection which has been enkindled in their children—Sperantus wants his son to marry Silena; Prisius wants his daughter to marry Accius. The children are unable to appreciate their fathers' efforts. Candius refuses to even listen to Sperantus; and Livia, one of the "new breed" of Elizabethan women, wants the privilege of selecting her own mate, a revolutionary idea whose dangers are readily apparent to Prisius: "Shee will choose with her eie, and like with her heart, before she consent with her tong; neither father nor mother, kith nor kin, shalbe her caruer in a husband, shee will fall too where she likes best; and thus the chicke scarce out of the shell, cackles as though she had bene troden with an hundreth cockes, and mother of a thousand egges" (50-55). The plotting of the fathers is momentarily interrupted by the appearance of their children, whereupon they retire to the side of the stage to spy.

The generation gap widens even further as Candius complains that his father respects only the intellects of old men and that he prefers profit to affection. Livia, who seconds Candius's criticisms,

adds that parents are nothing but selfish hypocrites. At the moment
the young lovers declare their undying affection, the fathers step
forth in all their paternal splendor; for, although Lyly's sympathies
lie ultimately with the lovers, he gives the fathers their just due.
They put the claims of parenthood very movingly as they express
their disappointment and anger at their children's total disregard
for their advice and feelings:

PRIS. And my minion hath wrought well, where euery stitch in her sampler
is a pricking stitch at my heart: you take your pleasure on parents, they are
peeuish, fooles, churles, ouergrowen with ignorance, because ouerworne
with age: litle shalt thou know the case of a father, before thy selfe be a
mother, when thou shalt breed thy childe with continuall paines, and
bringing it foorth with deadly pangs, nurse it with thine owne paps, and
nourish it vp with motherly tendernes; and then finde them to curse thee
with their hearts, when they shoulde aske blessing on their knees, and the
collop of thine owne bowels to be the torture of thine owne soul; with
teares trickling downe thy cheeks, and drops of bloud falling from thy
heart, thou wilt in vttering of thy minde wish them rather vnborne than vnnatural, & to haue had their cradles their graues rather than thy death their
bridals. But I will not dispute what thou shouldst haue done, but correct
what thou hast done: I perceiue sowing is an idle exercise, and that euerie
daie there come more thoughtes into thine head, than stitches into thy
worke; Ile see whether you can spin a better mind than you haue stitched,
and if I coope you not vp, then let me be the capon. *SPE.* As for you, sir
boy, in stead of poaring on a booke, you shall holde the plough; Ile make
repentance reape what wantonnesse hath sowen. But we are both well
serued: the sonnes must bee masters, the fathers gaffers; what wee get
together with a rake, they cast abroade with a forke; and wee must wearie
our legges to purchase our children armes. Well, seeing that booking is but
idlenesse, Ile see whether threshing be anie occupation: thy minde shall
stoope to my fortune, or mine shall break the lawes of nature. How like a
micher he standes, as though he had trewanted from honestie! Get thee in,
and for the rest let me alone. In villaine! (164-192)

Besides the elements noted, deception is important in Act I. In
the first two scenes, the fathers hide the idiocy of their progeny; in
the third scene, they spy on their children. The theme of deception
is doubly significant: (1) it will provide the nexus for a reversal of
the action later in the play when the deceivers will themselves be
deceived, and (2) it will serve as the turning point in Lyly's han-

dling of the appearance-versus-reality complex.

By the end of Act I, one might be tempted to view *Mother Bombie* as a standard Roman comedy, one complete with stereotyped characters—crusty fathers, clever servants, etc.—and with an erotic plot. But Lyly actually does something quite different from Plautus and Terence. As has just been seen, the fathers put the claims of parenthood in a more humane fashion than do their Roman counterparts; furthermore, the young lovers in Lyly's comedy are more complex creatures than are their Roman archetypes. Lyly, in short, humanizes the stock figures of Roman comedy.

Act II is constructed on an echo pattern, as the first two scenes are repeated by the last two; the third scene serves to separate the two groups. Throughout the act, plot and subplot are closely united as the four servants are followed about by their four masters. In Act II, Scene i, Dromio and Riscio meet, discover the similarity of their missions, and plot their own escapes. When Halfepenie enters with news that Sperantus and Prisius want to wed their children to those of Memphio and Stellio, his aid is elicited in playing a great trick on all of the fathers. They will arrange it so that Accius and Silena, the idiots, will marry, as well as Candius and Livia. Finally, Lucio enters and casts his lot with the others; and the scene ends with the four servants, who are in league against their four masters, engaged in a drinking song.

In Act II, Scene ii, Lyly briefly presents the obstacles which the four servants must overcome. The fathers arrive, each seeking his missing servant; and they retire to the same tavern into which the servants disappeared at the end of Act II, Scene i. The master-servant episode is interrupted in Act II, Scene iii, as Candius, acting on the instructions of his father, unenthusiastically agrees to woo Silena, whose idiocy is still unknown to him. Whatever Silena may lack in mentality, however, she makes up in physical attraction; and Candius falls in love with her at first sight. Here again Lyly employs an Elizabethan convention in an unconventional manner: love at first sight is the only love possible for Candius, for the moment that Silena opens her mouth she destroys the illusion her beauty has created, and Candius quickly falls out of love.

The remainder of the second scene is devoted to Mother Bombie, who is to this play what Madge Mumblecrust and the other rustics are to *Ralph Roister Doister*—a breath of merry old England in a

Roman setting. By occupation a fortune-teller, her particular specialty is palmistry; and when she reads Silena's palm, she reveals that the girl's parentage is in doubt; she is not, in fact, who she appears to be. Although Silena is too obtuse to grasp the implications of Mother Bombie's statement, the audience realizes that the way is being prepared for the marriage of Maestius and Serena, who, although presumably brother and sister, love each other. Mother Bombie is thus a manifestation of the convenient nanny who recognizes the strawberry birthmark on the heroine's left shoulder blade in the "lost-one-found" tradition of romance fiction.

The second act concludes with two short scenes devoted to the four servants (II.iv) and the four fathers (II.v). Having hatched their plot in the tavern, the servants reappear to set it in motion. The fathers, on the other hand, desirious of discovering how their servants have advanced the marriage plans, are eager to return to their homes. The plot thickens in the third act when two new characters—Maestius, son to Memphio and supposed son to Vicinia, and Serena, daughter to Stellio and supposed daughter to Vicinia—enter and introduce the incest theme. Believing themselves to be brother and sister, Maestius and Serena refuse to consummate their mutual passion. They do, however, lament over their unfortunate situation. In a speech that may have provided John Ford with a hint or two for '*Tis Pity She's a Whore* (1633), Maestius says: "The neerer we are in bloud, the further wee must be from loue; and the greater the kindred is, the lesse the kindnes must be; so that between brothers & sisters superstition hath made affection cold, between strangers custome hath bred loue exquisite" (20-24). When Serena suggests that they consult Mother Bombie, Maestius, though skeptical, agrees. When, after reading their palms, Mother Bombie declares that they will marry, without having sinned, on the morrow, they are convinced that she is mad.

By Act III, Scene ii, the plot of the servants has been set in motion; and Dromio has persuaded his master, Memphio, to lend him Accius's clothes so that he can find someone to impersonate the son in order to woo Silena. Riscio has likewise persuaded his master, Stellio, to lend him Silena's clothes so that he can find someone to impersonate the daughter in order to win Accius. When Halfepenie and Lucio enter, the real intention of Dromio and Riscio becomes apparent. Halfepenie reveals that he has got Candius and Livia to agree to send him their clothes. Although nothing explicit is said, the audience knows that Candius and Livia will impersonate Accius and Silena and thereby marry with their parents' unwitting consent. Accius and Silena now enter (III.iii) singing of Cupid and Venus; but their parents, who have followed them on stage and who hope to implement the servants' plot, call them away to their several homes. Both Memphio and Stellio believe that they are deceiving the other, but the audience knows differently. That both are being gulled by the servants is clearly evident from the action in Act III, Scene iv.

Halfepenie enters carrying the clothes of Candius and Lucio, and Rixula, a new servant girl, enters with the clothes of Livia. After a slightly bawdy passage between Rixula and the pages, Dromio and Riscio enter carrying the clothes of Accius and Silena. The disguise motif is momentarily set aside, however, as Lucio asks Mother Bombie to explain a dream which troubles him. The remainder of Act III, Scene iv. (83-192), is concerned with fortune-telling. In Act IV, Scene i, disguise becomes a means of illuminating the truth as Candius and Livia, disguised as Accius and Silena, convince their fathers, Prisius and Sperantus, that a marriage with the children of Memphio and Stellio is out of the question. Despite this turn of events, however, Prisius and Sperantus remain unalterably opposed to the union of their children. In contrast to Act IV, Scene i, where disguise was successful, it now fails (IV.ii) as the two idiot children, Accius and Silena, disguised as Candius and Livia, reveal to each other—and to each other's father—their idiocy. In disgust, the fathers blame Dromio and Riscio for the whole scheme.

At this point in the scene (IV.ii 167-402), Lyly introduces an irrelevancy in the form of a horse episode similar to one in Christopher Marlowe's *Dr. Faustus*.[18] Somewhere, sometime, Dromio has got into trouble with a hackneyman who now arrives with a sergeant to arrest Dromio for ruining a horse he had rented. The hackneyman agrees not to press his arrest when Riscio, Halfepenie, and Lucio post bond for Dromio.

The first two scenes of the fifth act prepare for the comic denouement of the third, and final, scene. In the first scene, the four servants are about to return to their masters in order to appease them and to conceal the marriage of Candius and Livia. The servants hope not only to escape a beating but also to win their freedom. In the second scene, Vicinia, who has for years concealed some terrible truth, comes to Mother Bombie to hear her fortune. Advised to unburden her conscience, Vicinia vows to reveal that she is the mother of Accius and Silena. The final scene (V.iii) is ushered in by fiddlers who come to play at a wedding reception. They try Sperantus's house first, but Candius sends them to Memphio, who in turn sends them packing. Realizing that no one is going to marry an idiot, except perhaps another idiot, Memphio leaves to arrange the details with Stellio. Meanwhile, Sperantus and Prisius discover that they have given their consent to their children's marriage. Then, after Riscio and Dromio reveal everything that has taken place, the idiot children are betrothed by their fathers. At this moment Vicinia arrives with the startling revelation that Accius and Silena are actually her children whom she had exchanged at birth for Memphio's son and Stellio's daughter, a revelation that can be proved by secret birthmarks. This revelation means, of course, that Maestius and Serena, hitherto believed to be brother and sister, are now free to marry. Finally, Memphio and Stellio offer to maintain Accius and Silena as they had been doing for years—besides, these two did not want to get married. In an additional burst of magnanimity, Memphio settles the suit that has been hanging over the head of Dromio. When the hackneyman, sergeant, and scrivener return to arrest Dromio, Memphio pays for the horse—and all's well that ends well.

In tragedy, the protagonist's misfortune must spring inevitably from his character and circumstances—coincidence weakens tragic action. Comedy, on the other hand, is composed of chances, changes, and surprises—coincidence heightens comic feeling. Susanne Langer defines comedy as an image of life triumphing over chance,[19] and her description is especially appropriate to Roman comedy, as well as its descendants, which is so often resolved by a last-minute discovery, with the assistance of a convenient nanny, that the prostitute or destitute maiden is actually the daughter of a prosperous citizen and therefore worthy of her young lover.

Mother Bombie presents an image of life triumphing over chance. Unfortunate in their idiocy, Accius and Silena are saved from an incestuous union by the fortunate discovery that they are brother and sister. Unfortunate in their supposed kinship, Maestius and Serena are joined in a happy union by the fortunate discovery that they are not related. Such fortunate discoveries occur through the fifth-act intervention of Vicinia, who appears in only one other scene in the play (V.ii). She just happens upon the scene, but comedy thrives upon such happenings, since wish-fulfillment rather than inevitability is its goal.

If *Mother Bombie* can be said to succeed as comedy, it does so on the basis of wish-fulfillment alone. Intrigue comedy, whether it be *Mother Bombie* or *Volpone*, is heavily dependent upon plot; for suspense is the play's principal element. Lyly, however, attempts to pour too much into the plot of *Mother Bombie*. He does not settle for one idiot child, but must have two; he is not satisfied with a pair of crusty fathers with children to wed, but must have four fathers, along with four children, not to mention four witty servants. Moreover, the initial intrigue is multiplied in such a labyrinthine fashion that suspense is soon sacrificed to confusion, and the comic catharsis is stillborn.

CHAPTER 6

The Plays and the Critics

I Negative Criticism

BECAUSE of the efforts of many contemporary critics, such as Jonas Barish and G. K. Hunter, Lyly's reputation as a dramatist has risen during the past twenty years. The modest enthusiasm he once received is represented by J. Dover Wilson's *John Lyly* (1905), the first full-length study. Wilson, who takes a conservative historical approach in his book, grants to Lyly the honor of having written the first English romantic drama. He refers to Lyly as the father of English comedy, and he claims that he excelled at the creation of female types who are the pivot of true comedy. Although Lyly's women—Sapho, the haughty; Mileta, the mocking; Gallathea, the demure; and Pipenetta, the saucy—"fill the English stage for the first time in history with their tears and their laughter, their scorn of the mere male and their 'curst yealding modestie,' their bold sallies and their bashful blushes," they are still without soul. They are husks of wit, raillery, and flirtation to Wilson; but then he asks, what of it? Unlike such earlier dramatic heroines as Dame Christian Custance in *Ralph Roister Doister* (1550), Lyly's women had wit. They are, Wilson concludes, "the Undines of our literature, beautiful and seductive, complete in everything but soul."[1]

Structurally, Wilson sees Lyly's comedies as evolving from the masque, and thus as partaking of the nature of pageantry, music, and pantomime. Also behind the comedies are the Medieval miracle and morality plays, especially the second. The morality, Wilson argues, separated drama and ritual by substituting typical or allegorical characters in place of the traditional religious figures of the miracle. Such plays served as either a positive indication of what life should be or as a negative indicator of what life is. In critical bent, the negative function leads more directly to comedy; and, when the criticism is combined with type characters, the movement toward comedy is doubly accelerated. Behind Lyly's comedies, then, lies the work of John Heywood, Nicholas Udall, Richard Edwards, and Edward Stevenson. Implicit in Wilson's analytical, historical approach is the concept that to understand Lyly is to understand these other writers as well. To appreciate Lyly's accomplishments is to read him against a background of late Medieval and early Renaissance drama.

The irony of Wilson's approach is that it creates the least enthusiastic response to the plays. On the one hand, it places a premium on plot and characterization—and finds Lyly wanting. On the other hand, it does little about modes of thought, or wit—elements that are only now attracting attention. Jocelyn Powell argues that the essence of Lyly's comedies is not found in plot or character but in mood. The emphasis is on figures of thought, on definition and exploration, on thinking—not on sensuous apprehension of reality. The emotional experience comes from involvement in different modes of being; and the plays are, in short, games for the mind.[2]

Wilson's approach has unwittingly diminished Lyly's reputation by stressing plot and characterization and by encouraging an examination of the plays as forerunners of Shakespeare's comedies. Interestingly enough, the most ardent of Lyly's contemporary critics, Peter Saccio, does not even mention Heywood, Udall, Edwards, or Stevenson. Instead of analyzing Lyly's comedies as forerunners of those of Shakespeare and others, Saccio sees them as the fulfillment of Sir Philip Sidney's desire for a comedy that "shoulde be full of delight."

Between Wilson and Saccio are a whole host of commentators who vary greatly in their responses and in their approaches to Lyly's comedies. In the first half of the twentieth century, histories of Elizabethan drama tended, because of their widespread use in colleges and universities, to create a stereotyped response toward Lyly. Characteristic is C. F. Tucker Brooke's *The Tudor Drama* (1911), which contends that Lyly, although the "first dominant personality that confronts the historian of the English drama," nevertheless wrote plays that "are marked by a striving for the unique and graceful at whatever cost to the plot."[3]

Somewhat later, but equally modest, are the claims made for Lyly's plays by Thomas M. Parrott and Robert H. Ball in *A Short View of Elizabethan Drama* (1943):

The action, in Lyly's plays, is anything but exciting. His plots, drawn for the most part from classical myth or legend, are simple and regular, but so slight that to fill up his orthodox five acts he has constant recourse to intercalary scenes in which minor characters divert the audience with song, with dancing, or with mockery of some ridiculous butt. . . . Not much can be said of Lyly's power of characterization. His people for the most part are stock types; the lover, the beloved, the coy mistress, the friend, and the intriguer; his women are graceful but almost lifeless figures.

Parrott and Ball have, to be sure, positive things to say about Lyly—"He set a pattern of witty speech and repartee in lively prose as the true vehicle of comic dialogue"—but the result of their study is negative.[4]

After listing Lyly's virtues, Ifor Evans, in *A Short History of English Drama* (1948), likewise includes Lyly in a list of dramatists whose popularity is ended. This book, like the others just cited, has had a wide circulation and has played, therefore, an important part in maintaining Lyly's reputation as a refined, delicate draftsman who is without substance.[5] More prestigious, and therefore more influential on serious students of Elizabethan drama, are the views expressed by T. W. Baldwin in his monumental *Shakspere's Five-Act Structure* (1947). Baldwin regards Lyly as a typical Terentian dramatist whose plays follow a set pattern. The first act presents the argument; the second begins the conflict; the third presents the epitasis; the fourth establishes the desperate situation brought about by the epitasis; the fifth leads to the catastrophe.[6] Baldwin's approach leads to a view of Lyly's plays as symmetrical dramas, a view supported by Zdenek Stríbrný, who argues that Lyly's Euphuism appears in his plays in the form of carefully balanced construction and antithetical groups of characters.[7]

Baldwin credits Lyly with the development of the love triangle. In *Campaspe*, it appears in a simplified form, for two men sue for the hand of one woman. In *Sapho and Phao*, Lyly inverts the triangle by having two women sue for the hand of one man. In *Gallathea*, he takes the next step by making all of his participants women. Not only does he make all of the participants women, but he has "doubled and interlocked his triangle." For each of the women disguised as a man he provides at least two rival women, one of whom is always the other disguised woman. But, in spite of the ingenuity and technical cleverness with which Baldwin credits Lyly, he is not overly enthusiastic. According to Baldwin, Lyly is unable to take meaningful advantage of the character conflicts which he creates in the comedies. "There is no motive force," Baldwin claims, "in the triangles; they are only for complication of the pattern." To Baldwin, Lyly excels only in structure; he is deficient in characterization.

II *Positive Criticism*

The approaches of Wilson and Baldwin are eschewed by most recent Lyly critics. In fact, Michael Best, after examining Lyly's comedies, arrives at a conclusion which sharply contradicts that of Baldwin.[9] Best argues that action is almost nonexistent in Lyly's plays, that the basic situation remains virtually unchanged throughout a play. In *Campaspe*, for example, Alexander's last words, "I will fall in loue," signifiy that the situation in the play which presented Alexander faced with the temptation of love has not really changed. *Sapho and Phao* ends where it begins; and *Endimion*, Best claims, "begins and ends with . . . the courtly lover hopelessly in love with the goddess, who graciously permits the love."[10] Such a view as this is possible, however, only when characterization is excluded from analysis; for the Endimion one leaves at the end of the play is quite a different character from the man met at the beginning.

A balanced view of Lyly's love comedies is presented by David L. Stevenson, who argues that romance had been rejected by Marston and Drayton, idealized beyond contamination from real life by Spenser, and described by Donne as the spiritual half of love, which in normal experience exists on both spititual and physical levels.[11] According to Stevenson, John Lyly was the first Elizabethan dramatist to realize that the opposed attitudes in this quarrel over romance could be effectively used on the stage. Although this critic does not credit Lyly with great powers of characterization—claiming that the characters do not ever come completely to life but simply voice current attitudes toward love—he does credit Lyly with originality in that he presented in dramatic form the complex love dilemma which was then fashionable in courtly circles. Lyly developed comedy to the point where characters exist not merely to relate a story but to act out the Elizabethan critical revolt from romance. Robert Y. Turner supports Stevenson's thesis by carrying it a step further.[12] Turner agrees that Lyly was the first English dramatist to present conversation which dramatizes love. Since Lyly created circumstances unfavorable to the lover's disclosure of his true sentiments, the lovers are forced to speak enigmatically, "in part from fear and in part from sensitivity to the delicate nature of love." This sensitivity Turner describes thus: "This tension between unfavorable circumstances and desire creates dialogue in which each assertion is tentative and each response quivering, and this dialogue, by not mentioning love directly, captures an unmistakable sense of what it is like to be in love, sometimes poignantly and sometimes wittily."[13]

Marco Mincoff veers in an opposite direction from that of Stevenson and Turner.[14] Mincoff suggests that in *Sapho and Phao* and *Gallathea*, Lyly had introduced as far as he was able the high love comedy of a delicate and subtle nature but that it was Shakespeare who developed it because he was not a court poet and was not drawn to the artificial code of love that ruled at court. Thus the love-game comedy which Stevenson sees as a comprehensive attitude toward romance Mincoff regards as only a small part of the whole. In short, Mincoff does not consider love or romance to be a game.

The search for the topical has long been a favorite pastime of Lyly critics, but little besides speculation has resulted. Allegorical equivalents are easy to discover, such as Cynthia's identification as Queen Elizabeth or Midas's identification as Prince Philip of Spain. Lately, however, the search for the allegorical has taken a new twist since critics have broadened their allegorical vision to include more universal forms. Bernard Huppé, for example, finds an allegory of love informing Lyly's comedies.[15] Huppé sees Lyly's conception of love in Euphues's declaration that true or virtuous love must be grounded upon time, reason, favor, and virtue. This conception, Huppé argues, lies at the heart of the allegory in *Sapho and Phao*, *Endimion*, *Love's Metamorphosis*, and *The Woman in the Moon*. In each of these plays the elements of the amoral and the moral, passion and chastity, are at strife; and chastity is fortified by the example of the Virgin Queen. Huppé's psychological reading puts the cart before the horse, argues Lyly's latest analyst, Peter Saccio.[16] Such approaches as Huppé's and P. W. Long's (who gives a Neoplatonic reading for *Endimion*) divest Renaissance allegory of its richness as gods and goddesses become merely costumed abstractions. To describe *Endimion* as " 'the "psychological" love story of Endimion, the courtly lover,' " and to read the gods as personifications of mental states, as Huppé does, is to place meaning before the fiction that creates the meaning.[17]

Paul A. Olson, who relates Shakespeare's *A Midsummer Night's Dream* to Lyly's court comedies, argues that Lyly's plays demand the sophistication of minds swift in catching emblematic meanings, a thesis also convincingly sustained by Huppé. For Lyly, the drama's patrons gave the drama laws; the laws were fixed by a court consistently interested in that art which builds its meaning from the materials of traditional emblems and allegories.[18]

What Jonas Barish has to say about *Euphues* and *Euphues and His England* is equally true of Lyly's plays. "If . . . logicality," Barish argues, "is once recognized as the basic principle of Lyly's style, the old difficulty of viewing the plays and the novels as part of a single stylistic system vanishes."[19] Barish claims for Lyly the role of revolutionary in the development of the language of comedy—a development as significant as Marlowe's development of the language was in tragedy. Barish does not view Lyly against Shakespeare; he considers him against a background composed of older vehicles of comedy such as Gascoigne's *Supposes* ("the clumsy, uncertain medium of Gascoigne's *Supposes*") and *The Famous Victories of Henry V* ("shambling, invertebrate language"). He concludes that "Lyly invented, virtually single-handed, a viable comic prose for the English stage. . . . For the first time, dramatic prose rested on an adequate structural foundation; for the first time, it was able to support an intricate plot without confusion and without prolixity,"[20] When Lyly is measured against his predecessors, he wins the prize for comedy; but as soon as he is measured against Shakespeare, his deficiencies immediately appear: "If, in his [Lyly's] passion for logicality, he evolved a style too rigid, too removed from common speech to lend itself easily to a wide range of effects, it was at the same time a style that needed only the further flexibility and modulation brought to it by Shakespeare to become an ideal dramatic prose."[21]

The rise in Lyly's reputation cited at the start of this chapter has not been entirely consistent. Voices are heard occasionally which echo those of Brooke, Parrott and Ball. As recently as 1962 Hereward T. Price could write: "Lyly never thought out the question of construction. . . . Lyly does not know what drama is."[22] Since 1962, however, criticism of Lyly's plays has been almost unanimous in its approval; and that year witnessed the publication of G. K. Hunter's *John Lyly: The Humanist as Courtier*. At the date of its publication, Hunter's book was the most comprehensive study available about Lyly's plays. After Hunter has analyzed each play separately, he concludes that Lyly's greatest strength lies in his ability to organize his material by two means: his patterned style and his mode of construction. Hunter isolates three of Lyly's unifying techniques: unification around debate (*Campaspe, Sapho and Phao, Endimion, Midas*); harmonious variety (*Gallathea, Loves Metamorphosis, The Woman in the Moon*); and subplot intrigue (*Mother Bombie*). This approach to the plays, though critically advantageous, neglects chronology; and it also leads Hunter to make some unusual observations, such as suggesting that *Endimion* represents a development from *Midas*, a later play by Hunter's own dating.[23]

Hunter uses the theme of appearance and reality in a fresh manner by applying it to Lyly's own artistic philosophy. According to Hunter, Lyly was aware that his plays were "unreal." For Lyly, his courtly audience was the reality and the fount of truth; therefore, his plays could only approach truth by mirroring the court's virtues and could be at best but a shadow of that true perfection.

Ultimately, Hunter's categories are based on logical rather than real distinctions. Although the debate plays an important role in *Campaspe*, it also does so in *The Woman in the Moon*, a play which is included in the classification "harmonious variety." This categorization in itself is somewhat ironic, in that *Woman in the Moon* is Lyly's only play with a single story line. *Mother Bombie* can be justly included in the classification "subplot intrigue"—but so can *Midas*, which has a more complicated subplot structure than *Mother Bombie*, which can be discussed just as well as a play unified around debate or through harmonious variety. As long as the reader takes Hunter's classifications lightly, they can be helpful in illustrating the structure of Lyly's plays. If too great an emphasis is placed upon his classifications, they simply confuse what is already sufficiently obscure.

Hunter's more speculative judgment that Lyly tried in his plays to mirror the virtue of the court and that the plays themselves are but a shadow of the court's perfection is not borne out by the texts. Too often Lyly operates as a satirist or he too often finds fault with courtly virtues for such a judgment to stand. In *Campaspe*, for example, Parmenio, speaking about monarchs, says: "They haue long eares and stretched armes, in whose heades suspition is a proofe, and to be accused is to be condemned" (III.iv.6-8). Similarly, in *Sapho and Phao* (III.iii), Sapho is presented as caught in the grip of an overwhelming passion, as writhing and tossing on her hot bed of celibacy. Such instances as these, and there are many others, argue against Hunter's assumptions about Lyly's esthetic orientation.

Although not the most comprehensive, Peter Saccio's *The Court Comedies of John Lyly* is the most detailed analysis of Lyly's court comedies. Whereas Hunter devotes about one hundred octavo pages to a discussion of all eight of the comedies, Saccio devotes about two hundred to five plays. Saccio is by far the most enthusiastic Lyly admirer who has appeared on the critical scene. His claims for Lyly's genius surpass those of Hunter, or even those of R. W. Bond, Lyly's early twentieth-century editor.

Saccio, who approaches Lyly from the point of view of structure, argues that in the five court comedies—*Campaspe, Sapho and Phao, Gallathea, Endimion,* and *Love's Metamorphosis*—the dramatic structure assumes the form of allegorical frames. Saccio, who quite rightly differentiates between structure and plot, agrees that the plots are slight; but, to appreciate Lyly, Saccio claims that one must understand his use of dramaturgical techniques which have not been "adequately described."[24] In Saccio's pursuit of an adequate description, he eschews the methods of his predecessors; for he contends that Baldwin forces Lyly's dramaturgy into a Roman scheme, although, except for *Mother Bombie*, Lyly wrote no Roman comedies, and that G. K. Hunter, although performing a useful function by discarding the older and confusing labels attached to Lyly's comedies—historical, allegorical, pastoral, and realistic—nevertheless does not come to grips with the contents of the plays.

What is required, Saccio concludes, is a thorough analysis of all of the dramatic elements—acts, scenes, speeches, props, images, themes—if Lyly is to be seen in anything like his true place in English drama. Finally, Saccio argues, greater attention must be paid to the allegory; but Saccio does not mean by "allegory" what his predecessors meant. He does not mean the search for the topical that began in the nineteenth century and stretched as far into the present as Josephine W. Bennett's 1942 article, "Oxford and Endimion."[25] According to Saccio, allegory "is not a form but a mode of literary operation, a stimulation of larger senses of meaning from the literal sense of the play, an interaction between the play and its audience."[26]

In a chapter entitled "A Stage for Allegory," Saccio explains the staging of Lyly's plays; and the critic does so partly to combat such popular misconceptions, fostered by R. W. Bond among others, as the notion that Lyly's plays were staged in the manner of the popular Elizabethan theater and partly to explain his own approach to allegory. Saccio's conclusion is a key to the critical method which he employs in his examination of the individual plays: "The Lylian stage picture precisely fulfills the conventional Elizabethan definition of allegory: the stage picture is a continued metaphor. Lyly's stage, with its juxtaposition of symbols in a pattern to be animated by the words and deeds of the characters, is a stage for allegory."[27]

Although Saccio realizes that a play exists in time and space, he is predisposed to examine it as if it were a poem existing in eternity. He betrays himself when—in discussing the narrative line of progression in drama and its relative absence in Lyly's plays—he suggests that the static quality of the private stage effects a somewhat similar quality in the plays. He writes that "on a stage ever the same because of the fixed houses, the seen actors and properties move back and forth creating an unseen reality." In Lyly's plays, if I read Saccio correctly, one does not have an insistence upon emotional excitement contingent upon following a line of related experiences. Instead, one has "a central reality slowly turning like a prism for us to inspect its various facets."[28] But a play is not like a prism, solid and fixed on a single axis, that turns slowly so one can examine its every facet. Drama does not stand still—not for the spectators, not for the critic—neither does it move in slow motion. Drama, above all, is restless; conflict, by its very nature, partakes of the active forces of life.

Perhaps the best description of dramatic activity remains J. Dover Wilson's: "Above all it [Elizabethan drama] was action in motion, a work of art which, unlike that of architecture, sculpture, painting, or lyrical poetry, was not to be apprehended in all its parts at one and the same moment, but conveyed the intentions of its creator through a *series* of impressions, each fleeting as the phases of a musical symphony, each deriving tone and colour from all that had gone before and bestowing tone and colour on all that came after, and each therefore contributing to the cumulative effect which was only felt when the play was completed."[29]

CHAPTER 7

Lyly's Reputation and Influence

I Lyly the Stylist

JOHN Lyly was a phenomenon during his lifetime and a legacy after his death. Although considered the most fashionable English writer of the 1580's, Lyly had by 1600 become an object of ridicule. Subsequent writers, such as Sir Philip Sidney,[1] were to maintain the dignity and relevance of an artificial prose style; but the degree of elaboration which infused Lyly's prose could not survive the threats posed by the new logic of Petrus Ramus and a growing, literate middle class.[2] John Dryden is not called the "father" of modern English prose for nothing, for one witnesses in his polished yet straightforward sentences the resolution which ultimately pointed English prose down a middle path between the artificiality of Lyly and the naturalness of Thomas Deloney.

In terms of both form and content John Lyly left his mark on subsequent English narrative and comedy. The success of *Euphues* and *Euphues and His England* occasioned a succession of Euphuistic romances, including such notable successes as Greene's *Pandosto* (1588) and Lodge's *Rosalynde* (1590), which is subtitled *Euphues Golden Legacy*. Lyly's insistence in his comedies upon the importance of mythological and pastoral characters and settings certainly influenced the early Shakespeare, for *A Midsummer Night's Dream* and *As You Like It* both bear the print of Lyly's handiwork. But English comedy was not destined to follow the lead of either Lyly or Shakespeare: the mythological and the pastoral gave way to the bourgeois and the drawing room when Ben Jonson and the Restoration dramatists established the comedy of manners as the quintessential English type.

Though Lyly's influence in comedy was not pervasive, it was nevertheless impressive. English comic prose written before Lyly was subject to the same flaws that characterize much sixteenth-century poetry, especially that written during the third quarter, as the following lines from Sackville's "Induction" to *The Mirror for Magistrates* illustrate:

> O Sorrow, alas, sith Sorrow is thy name,
> And that to thee this drear doth well pertain,
> In vain it were to seek to cease the same. (134-136) [3]

George Gascoigne would have, no doubt, given high marks to Sackville's verse, for it embodies one of Gascoigne's principal rules of composition: "Here by the way I thinke it not amisse to forewarne you that you thrust as few wordes of many sillables into your verse as may be: add herevnto I might alledge many reasons. First, the most auncient English wordes are of one sillable, so that the more monasyllables that you vse the truer Englishman you shall seeme, and the lesse you shall smell of the Inkehorne: Also wordes of many syllables do cloye a verse and make it vnpleasant, . . ."[4]

Gascoigne practiced what he preached. His lyric "Amid my bale I bathe in bliss" contains 254 words, 221 of which are monosyllables.[5] His injunction carried over into his comic prose, which is likewise overloaded with little words. But, as Jonas Barish points out, "the tendency to load down his sentences with heaps of little words would matter less if it were not linked to a persistent preference for clumsy connectives, unwieldly constructions involving auxiliary clauses, and in general a preference for a roundabout rather than a direct way of stating a thing."[6]

Lyly does not load his sentences with "heaps of little words." Neither does he employ clumsy connectives, nor does he sidle around statements like a crab, turning simple statements into winding, circuitous syntactic journeys.[7] A singular irony exists, therefore, in the fact that Lyly's most famous contribution to literature—his Euphuistic prose style—was ultimately the reason for his eclipse. Critics have been quick to point out Lyly's use of antithesis and parallelism and his fondness for involved images and allusions drawn from unnatural natural history and mythology. Few critics, however, have been eager to discuss Lyly's logicality.[8] That the logicality is present is obvious; that it plays second fiddle to the style is equally obvious.

Euphuistic style, in short, calls attention to itself. Although no clear distinction between form and content can be drawn, one can be stressed at the expense of the other, as anyone can attest who has listened to a satisfied grunt of an infant. When the form so clearly calls attention to itself as Lyly's does, the content suffers. The point of view suggested by the title of Jocelyn Powell's "John Lyly and the Language of Play" is more easily understood than is a recognition of Lyly's logicality.[9] Lyly does appear to be making a game of style, for one can follow the convolutions of his syntax with something of the same delight experienced by a child watching a dog chasing its own tail.

Until the last twenty years or so, a period during which rhetorical analyses have become current, the usual critical attitude toward Lyly's style was that it was elegant but little more. This verdict is understandable but unjust. Lyly's use of antithesis, often in the form of paradox, may bedazzle readers unused to rhetorical brilliance; but no figure can more effectively illustrate the complexity of Lyly's ironic vision of reality.

II *Lyly the Romanticist*

Apart from style, Lyly's influence can be felt in the romantic comedies written in the 1590's. Although Lyly was not the "father of English comedy,"[10] he was the progenitor of a comic form which intermingled divine intervention and human craving for love and affection, a form which leads ultimately to *A Midsummer Night's Dream* and, perhaps, even to *The Tempest*. More important than his form, however, is Lyly's presentation of female characters on the English stage. Before Lyly wrote, English drama had a tendency to minimize women's roles. The morality drama focused almost exclusively on male characters. In *All for Money* (1577), for example, Thomas Lupton altered his source in order to eliminate female roles: he keeps offstage a woman infanticide (she communicates by letter), and he changes the sex of a criminal who was a woman in his source.[11] But such was not the case with the mystery plays, which, by their very nature, had to present characterizations of women on stage. But even in them the number of roles was few, consisting mainly of Eve; Noah's wife; Mary, the mother of Jesus; Mary Magdalen; and the grieving mothers of the slaughtered infants.

Only Eve is a participant in an erotic relationship, and the force of it is negative.

Because records are so scanty, one finds it virtually impossible to say anything definite about romantic comedy before Lyly.[12] To be sure, plays were written on subjects that would lend themselves to romantic treatment, such as the Troilus story; but most such dramas are lost. Even in extant plays that are derived from sources that are themselves romantic, the female roles are reduced to a minimum. George Gascoigne's *Supposes* (c. 1565), for example, is an imitation of Ariosto's *Suppositi* (c. 1509), an Italianate love-intrigue comedy, yet Gascoigne does not permit his lovers to meet upon the stage before the closing lines, and they never speak to each other.[13]

Lyly's Campaspe, Sapho, and Gallathea may not be the Undines of English literature, as J. Dover Wilson claims,[14] but they are a far cry from the passive heroines that earlier populated the English stage. Lyly's heroines love and hate, cry and laugh; they are desirable yet often unapproachable; they are intolerably demanding yet often tenderly yielding. They represent not merely woman loved but woman in love; and they stand, therefore, as the precursors of dramatic romantic heroines from Shakespeare's Rosalind to Shaw's Liza Doolittle.

John Lyly lost his appeal to the English imagination near the end of the sixteenth century. Like his contemporary Thomas Lodge, who rejected writing in favor of medicine, Lyly chose politics, retired to country life, and died in 1606—all but ignored by the literary world which earlier had acclaimed him as its brightest star.

Notes and References

Chapter One

1. John Lyly, *Euphues, the Anatomy of Wit* and *Euphues and His England*, ed. Morris W. Croll and Harry Clemons (London, 1916; reprint 1964), p. 232. All subsequent references to the prose narratives are to this edition. References to the plays are to R. Warwick Bond, *The Complete Works of John Lyly*, 3 vols. (Oxford, 1902; reprint 1967). Wherever possible, page numbers are included in the text.

2. William Ringler, "The Immediate Source of Euphuism," *Publications of the Modern Language Association*, LIII (1938), 678-686.

3. Quoted in G. K. Hunter, *John Lyly: The Humanist as Courtier* (London, 1962), p. 41.

4. Leslie Hotson, ed., *Queen Elizabeth's Entertainment at Mitcham* (New Haven, 1953), attributes the work to Lyly, but few critics agree. The opposition is represented by Kenneth Muir, review of *Queen Elizabeth's Entertainment at Mitcham* by Leslie Hotson in *Review of English Studies*, V (1954), 407-409.

5. Hardin Craig, ed., *I Henry IV*, in *The Complete Works of Shakespeare* (Chicago, 1961), II. iv.438ff.

6. Francis Meres, *Palladis Tamia* (1598), in *Ancient Critical Essays upon English Poets and Poësy*, ed. Joseph Haslewood, II (London, 1815), 154.

7. Quoted in John Buxton, *Sir Philip Sidney and the English Renaissance*, 2nd ed. (London, 1964), p. 9.

8. *Ibid.*, p. 10.

9. Walter Davis, *Sidney's Arcadia* (New Haven, 1965), p. 57.

10. G. B. Harrison, ed., *Shakespeare: The Complete Works* (New York, 1952), p. 33.

11. C. S. Lewis, *English Literature in the Sixteenth Century* (London, 1954), p. 312.

12. More recent studies include G. K. Hunter's *John Lyly* (1962) and Peter Saccio's *Ohe Court Comedies of John Lyly* (Princeton, 1969).

13. Jonas Barish, "The Prose Style of John Lyly," *English Literary History*, XXIII (1956), 16.

14. *Ibid.*, p. 24.

15. Geoffrey Tillotson, "The Prose Style of Lyly's Comedies," in *Essays in Criticism and Research* (Cambridge, 1942), p. 22.

16. Zdenek Stríbrný, "John Lyly a Dvorské Drama," *Philologica Pragensia*, VI (1963), 100-112.

17. Barish, "Prose Style," p. 34.

18. Saccio, *Court Comedies*, p. 43.

19. *Ibid.*, p. 51.

20. *Ibid.*

Chapter Two

1. See, for example, Edd W. Parks, "Before *Euphues*," in *Joseph Quincy Adams: Memorial Studies*, ed. James G. McManaway, *et al.* (Washington, 1948), pp. 475-493.

2. Hunter, *John Lyly*, pp. 55-56.

3. Steven Gosson, *The Schoole of Abuse* (1579), in *English Literary Criticism: The Renaissance*, ed. O. B. Hardison, Jr. (New York, 1963), p. 87.

4. Hardin Craig, ed., *Machiavelli's The Prince: An Elizabethan Translation* (Chapel Hill, 1944). Machiavelli's anonymous Elizabethan translator puts it thus: "Therefore itt is verie necessarie for a prince to knowe as well howe to use the force and subtilty of beastes, as the faythe and sincerenes of men ' (p. 75).

5. J. Dover Wilson, "Euphues and the Prodigal Son," *Library*, N.S. X (1909), p. 337.

6. The "Cooling Card" is a selective paraphrase of Ovid's *Remedia Amoris*, with a short introduction and conclusion and some interjection of Lyly's own composition, says Albert Feuillerat, *John Lyly: Contribution à l'Histoire de la Renaissance en Angleterre* (Cambridge, 1910), Appendix C, pp. 583-594.

7. The "Euphues and His Ephebus" section is indebted to Plutarch's *De Educatione Puerorum* (Bond, I, 352n) and to Erasmus's *Colloquium Puerpera (Euphues*, ed. Croll and Clemons, p. 111n.).

8. Although the grandson of William Lily, the famous Humanist grammarian, John Lyly advances none of the Humanist educational reforms except those which it incidentally shared with Classical antiquity. Never, for instance, does Lyly emphasize increased education for women, a matter of considerable importance to earlier English Humanists such as Sir Thomas More.

9. See Bond, *Complete Works*, I, 364ff., for the theological content of the dialogue.

10. This form of conclusion had been popularized by Guevara, whose *Libro Aureo* ends with "Certain Letters written by M. Aurelius," and was reproduced with this title in North's *Diall of Princes* (1557)—cf. *Euphues*, ed. Croll and Clemons, p. 163.

11. Peter Ure, ed., *King Richard II*, 4th ed. (Cambridge, Mass., 1956), pp. 21n.-22n.

12. Cf. *Euphues*, ed. Croll and Clemons, p. 179n.

13. *Ibid.*, p. 200n.

14. Boccaccio's *Il Filocolo* (c. 1338) and Bembo's *Asolani* (1505) were the most influential predecessors of Castiglione's *Il Cortegiano* (1528), translated in 1561 by Sir Thomas Hoby under the title *The Courtier*.

15. See Chapter Seventeen of *The Prince* entitled "Of crueltie and gentlenes, and whether it be better to be loved or Feared" (Craig edition, pp. 71-74).

16. Euphues's "Glass for Europe" is derived from William Harrison's *Description of England* (1577).

Chapter Three

1. On the "intermediate" morality plays, see David Bevington, *From Mankind to Marlowe* (Cambridge, Mass., 1962).

2. Glynne Wickham, *Early English Stages*, I (London, 1963), 80.

3. On the subject matter and thematic content of Roman comedy, see Erich Segal, *Roman Laughter: The Comedy of Plautus* (Cambridge, Mass., 1968; reprint 1971), p. 93.

4. Saccio, *Court Comedies*, pp. 225-226.

5. An extensive plot summary of *Alexander and Campape* can be found in Karl J. Holzknecht, *Outlines of Tudor and Stuart Play: 1497-1642* (New York, 1947), pp. 42-45.

6. J. Dover Wilson, *John Lyly* (Cambridge, 1905), p. 101.

7. Hereward T. Price, "Shakespeare and His Young Count emporaries," *Philological Quarterly*, XLI (1962), 40-41.

8. Hunter, *John Lyly*, p. 163.

9. Saccio, *Court Comedies*, p. 32.

10. *Ibid.*, p. 93.

11. *Ibid.*, pp. 26-27.

12. *Ibid.*, p. 38.

13. *Ibid.*, p. 93.

14. *Ibid.*, pp. 93-94.

15. *Campaspe*, I.i, iii; II.ii; III.iv; V.iv.

154

JOHN LYLY

16. *Ibid.*, III.iv.
17. *Ibid.*, 196-260.
18. *Ibid.* (nine versus five).
19. *Ibid.*, III.v. 13-61.
20. Saccio, *Court Comedies*, p. 31.
21. *Ibid.*, p. 2.
22. Hunter, *John Lyly*, p. 165.
23. John Leon Lievsay, "Some Renaissance Views of Diogenes the Cynic," *Joseph Quincy Adams: Memorial Studies*, p. 453.
24. *Campaspe*, I.i. 69-79.
25. On the problem of the songs in Lyly's plays, see Hunter, *John Lyly*, pp. 367-372.
26. Nicholas Udall, *Ralph Roister Doister*, in *The English Drama 900-1642*, ed. Edd W. Parks and Richmond C. Beatty (New York, 1935), pp. 125-26.
27. Hunter, *John Lyly*, pp. 14-15.
28. *Ibid.*, pp. 160-161.
29. Saccio, *Court Comedies*, p. 78.
30. On this point, see David M. Bevington, "John Lyly and Queen Elizabeth: Royal Flattery in *Campaspe* and *Sapho and Phao*," *Renaissance Papers 1966*, ed. George W. Williams (1967), pp. 57-67.
31. On the allegory in *Campaspe*, see Hunter, *John Lyly*, pp. 166-177, and Bernard Huppé, "Allegory of Love in Lyly's Court Comedies," *English Literary History*, XIV (1947), 93-113.
32. Bond, *Complete Works*, III, 20.
33. Wilson, *John Lyly*, p. 125.
34. T. W. Baldwin, *Shakespeare's Five-Act Structure* (Urbana, 1947), p. 503.
35. Barish, "Prose Style," p. 34.
36. See, for example, Philautus's lament about Lucilla's desertion to Euphues (*Euphues*, ed. Croll and Clemons, p. 73).
37. Noted by Bond, *Complete Works*, II, 559n.
38. Robert Y. Turner, "Some Dialogues of Love in Lyly's Comedies," *English Literary History*, XXIX (1962), 279.

Chapter Four

1. The importance of setting to *Gallathea* is discussed by Anne B. Lancashire, ed., *Gallathea* and *Midas* (Lincoln, Nebraska, 1969), p. xviii.
2. Saccio, *Court Comedies*, p. 98.
3. *Ibid.*, p. 160.
4. *Ibid.*, pp. 99ff.
5. For a similar handling, see Erasmus's "Alchemy," in *Ten Colloquies*,

ed. Craig R. Thompson, (New York, 1957), pp. 47-55.

6. Bond, *Complete Works*, 570-571n.

7. Stone in the sense "testicle."

8. Lancashire, *Gallathea*, p. xxvi.

9. On love analysis in *Endimion*, see David L. Stevenson, *The Love-Game Comedy* (London, 1946), pp. 159-162.

10. An extended plot summary of *Endimion* can be found in *Outlines of Tudor and Stuart Plays*, pp. 45-50.

11. N. J. Halpin, *Oberon's Vision in the Midsummer-Night's Dream, Illustrated by a Comparison with Lylie's Endymion* (London, 1843); Josephine W. Bennett, "Oxford and Endimion," *Publications of the Modern Language Association*, LVII (1942), 354-369.

12. See Bond, *Complete Works*, III, 10, for a detailed list of correspondences.

13. Huppé, "Allegory of Love," p. 103.

14. J. A. Bryant, Jr., "The Nature of the Allegory in Lyly's *Endymion*," *Renaissance Papers 1956*, ed. Hennig Cohen and J. Woodrow Hassell, Jr. (1957), pp. 4-11, disagrees with Huppé's Platonic interpretation and advances a Christian allegorical explanation.

15. J. W. H. Atkins, *English Literary Criticism: the Renascence* (London, 1947), pp. 240-241.

16. See Hunter, *John Lyly*, pp. 42ff.

17. Andreas Capellanus, *The Art of Courtly Love*, ed. Frederick W. Locke (New York, 1957), pp. 42-43.

18. *Ralph Roister Doister*, III.iii.

19. For a detailed description of the typical Elizabethan beauty, see Lu Emily Pearson, *Elizabethan Love Conventions* (Berkeley, 1933), pp. 325-326.

20. In the early comedies of Shakespeare, such as *The Two Gentlemen of Verona* and *The Merchant of Venice*, the convention obtained, but in later comedies such as *Much Ado About Nothing* and *The Winter's Tale* it collapsed in the face of pressures imposed by Renaissance theories of love.

21. Saccio, *Court Comedies*, p. 163.

22. Bond, *Complete Works*, II.i.15, 29. A stage direction places her in V.i, but no lines are assigned to her.

23. Both Huppé, "Allegory of Love," p. 107, and Hunter, *John Lyly*, p. 205, claim that the foresters represent the Petrarchan poet-lover; and the three nymphs, three aspects of the Petrarchan unkind mistress, alternately cruel, coy, and inconstant.

24. Michael Best, "Lyly's Static Drama," *Renaissance Drama*, N.S. I (1968), 80, argues that Protea and Petulus achieve happiness only because their capacity for love enables them to accept and forgive imperfection.

25. Paul Parnell, "Moral Allegory in Lyly's *Loves Metamorphosis,*" *Studies in Philology*, LII (1955), 1-16, offers a different interpretation of the play.

Chapter Five

1. Baldwin, *Five-Act Structure*, p. 536, argues that, because of its two-plot structure, *Midas* is the poorest of Lyly's dramas. Lyly is defended by Michael Best, "A Theory of the Literary Genesis of Lyly's *Midas,*" *Review of English Studies*, N.S. XVII (1966), 133-140, who advances a theory that Lyly had earlier written two separate plays about Midas and later combined them. Hunter, *John Lyly*, pp. 177-184, includes *Midas* in the group of plays unified around debate.

2. See Don C. Allen, "A Note on Lyly's *Midas*, II," *Modern Language Notes*, LXI (1946), 503-504, for information about the cosmic egg.

3. See the explanatory notes to Anne B. Lancashire's edition of *Midas*.

4. Wilson, *John Lyly*, p. 124.

5. Anne B. Lancashire, *Gallathea* and *Midas*, pp. xxii-xxiii, sees *Midas* as a clear allegory in which Midas represents Philip II of Spain; Phrygia, Spain; Lesbos, England; and Midas's touch, the gold returning to Spain from her colonies. She suggests, however, that the moral nature of the play is more important than the political allegory.

6. Bond, *Complete Works*, III, 233.

7. Johnstone Parr, "Astrology Motivates a Comedy," in *Tamburlaine's Malady and Other Essays on Astrology in Elizabethan Drama* (Tuscaloosa, Alabama, 1953), pp. 38-49.

8. Baldwin, *Five-Act Structure*, pp. 518-519.

9. Bond, *Complete Works*, III, p. 236.

10. Huppé, "Allegory of Love," pp. 111ff.

11. Hunter, *John Lyly*, p. 219.

12. Best, "Lyly's Static Drama," p. 82.

13. Saccio, *Court Comedies*, p. 204.

14. Barish, "Prose Style," pp. 21-23.

15. Best, "Lyly's Static Drama," pp. 84-85.

16. Baldwin, *Five-Act Structure*, pp. 530-531.

17. Hunter, *John Lyly*, pp. 220-229.

18. Christopher Marlowe, *Doctor Faustus*, ed. Roma Gill (New York, 1965), IV.v.

19. Susanne K. Langer, *Feeling and Form* (New York, 1953), p. 348.

Chapter Six

1. Wilson, *John Lyly*, p. 126.

2. Jocelyn Powell, "John Lyly and the Language of Play," *Elizabethan Theatre*, ed. John R. Brown and Bernard Harris (London, 1966), pp. 147-167.

3. C. F. Tucker Brooke, *The Tudor Drama* (Boston, 1911), pp. 172-173.

4. Thomas M. Parrott and Robert H. Ball, *A Short View of Elizabethan Drama* (New York, 1943), pp. 65, 66.

5. Ifor Evans, *A Short History of English Drama*, 2nd ed. (Boston, 1965), pp. 42-43.

6. Baldwin, *Five-Act Structure*, p. 497.

7. Stríbrný, "John Lyly," pp. 100-112.

8. Baldwin, *Five-Act Structure*, p. 509.

9. Best, "Lyly's Static Drama," pp. 75-86.

10. *Ibid.*, p. 76.

11. Stevenson, *Love-Game Comedy*, pp. 148-173.

12. Turner, "Some Dialogues of Love," pp. 276-288.

13. *Ibid.*, p. 279.

14. Marco Mincoff, "Shakespeare and Lyly," *Shakespeare Survey*, 14 (1961), 15-24.

15. Huppé, "Allegory of Love," pp. 93-113.

16. Saccio, *Court Comedies*, p. 7.

17. *Ibid.*, pp. 104-105.

18. Paul A. Olson, "*A Midsummer Night's Dream* and the Meaning of Court Marriage," *English Literary History*, XXIV (1957), 95-119.

19. Barish, "Prose Style," p. 27.

20. *Ibid.*, p. 34.

21. *Ibid.*, p. 35.

22. Price, "Shakespeare and His Young Contemporaries," pp. 40-41.

23. Noted by Harold Jenkins, review of *John Lyly: The Humanist as Courtier*, by G. K. Hunter, *Modern Language Review*, LIX (1964), 104-106.

24. Saccio, *Court Comedies*, p. 2.

25. Bennett, "Oxford and Endimion," pp. 354-369.

26. Saccio, *Court Comedies*, p. 5.

27. *Ibid.*, p. 25.

28. *Ibid.*, p. 190.

29. J. Dover Wilson, *What Happens in Hamlet* (Cambridge, 1935), p. 230.

Chapter Seven

1. Although a noted stylist, Sidney was less than enthusiastic about certain features of Euphuism, especially the unnatural natural history (*An*

Apology for Poetry, ed. Geoffrey Shepherd [London, 1965], p. 139).

2. For a discussion of the effects of Ramus's logic on English prose, see Walter J. Ong, "Tudor Writings on Rhetoric," *Studies in the Renaissance*, XV (1968), 39-69.

3. Hyder E. Rollins and Herschel Baker, eds., *The Renaissance in England* (Boston, 1954), p. 273.

4. George Gascoigne, *Certayne Notes of Instruction*, in *English Literary Criticism: The Renaissance*, ed. O. B. Hardison, Jr. (New York, 1963), p. 78.

5. Rollins and Baker, *Renaissance in England*, p. 302.

6. Jonas A. Barish, *Ben Jonson and the Language of Prose Comedy* (Cambridge, Mass., 1960), p. 7.

7. *Ibid.*, p. 8.

8. Even though Jonas A. Barish has modified, or reversed, many of the older, historical attitudes toward Euphuism, their persistence can be witnessed in Lyly's latest editor, Anne B. Lancashire, who refers her readers to Croll and Clemons, not to Barish, for a discussion of Lyly's style.

9. See Chapter Six, pp. 137-146.

10. J. Dover Wilson, *John Lyly*, p. 125.

11. Bevington, *From Mankind to Marlowe*, p. 75.

12. See F. P. Wilson, *The English Drama 1485-1585*, ed. G. K. Hunter (Oxford, 1969), p. 111.

13. *Ibid.*, p. 115.

14. Wilson, *John Lyly*, p. 126.

Selected Bibliography

PRIMARY SOURCES

The best complete edition of Lyly's two prose narratives is *Euphues, the Anatomy of Wit* and *Euphues and his England*, ed. Morris W. Croll and Harry Clemons. London: Routledge and Kegan Paul, 1916 (reissued, Russell & Russell, 1964). The best complete edition of Lyly's plays is *The Complete Works of John Lyly*, ed. R. Warwick Bond. 3 Vols. Oxford: Clarendon Press, 1902 (reprinted 1967). These two editions are referred to throughout this volume. A list of first editions follows:

Euphues, the Anatomy of Wit. London, 1578.
Euphues and His England. London, 1580.
Alexander and Campaspe. London, 1584.
Sapho and Phao. London, 1584.
Endimion. London, 1591.
Gallathea. London, 1592.
Midas. London, 1592.
Mother Bombie. London, 1594.
The Woman in the Moon. London, 1597.
Love's Metamorphosis. London, 1601.

The reader may also wish to consult the following works:

Blount, Edward, ed. *Sixe Court Comedies.* London, 1632. The earliest edition of the plays.

Fairholt, F. W., ed. *The Dramatic Works of John Lyly.* 2 vols. London, 1858.

Houppert, Joseph W. "John Lyly," in *The Predecessors of Shakespeare*, ed. Terence P. Logan and Denzell S. Smith. Lincoln, Nebraska: University of Nebraska Press, 1973, pp. 125-142. Contains a discussion of the Lyly canon, including uncertain ascriptions.

Lancashire, Anne, ed. *Midas* and *Gallathea.* Lincoln, Nebraska: University of Nebraska Press, 1969.

Lawless, Merritt, ed. *Euphues, The Anatomy of Wit*, in *Elizabethan Prose Fiction*. New York: Odyssey Press, 1967, pp. 113-188.

SECONDARY SOURCES

BALDWIN, T. W. *Shakspere's Five-Act Structure*. Urbana: University of Illinois Press, 1947. Attempts to view Lyly's plays in terms of traditional five-act, Roman comic form.

BARISH, JONAS A. "The Prose Style of John Lyly," *English Literary History*, XXIII (1956), 14-35. Penetrating examination of Euphuism which emphasizes its paradoxical nature.

BEST, MICHAEL R. "A Theory of the Literary Genesis of Lyly's *Midas*," *Review of English Studies*, N.S. XVII (1966), 133-140. Presents an unconvincing argument that *Midas* is actually a composite play formed from two earlier versions.

―――――. "Lyly's Stratic Drama," *Renaissance Drama*, N.S. I (1968), 75-86. Emphasizes theme at the expense of plot and characterization.

BOUGHNER, DANIEL C. "The Background of Lyly's Tophas," *Publications of the Modern Language Association*, LIV (1939), 967-973. Indicates Italian and Latin parallels to the words and actions of Lyly's Tophas.

BRADBROOK, M. C. *The Growth and Structure of Elizabethan Comedy*. Baltimore: Penguin Books, 1963. Useful general introduction to the subject.

BRYANT, J. A., JR. "The Nature of the Allegory in Lyly's *Endymion*," *Renaissance Papers 1956*, ed. Hennig Cohen and J. Woodrow Hassell, Jr. Durham: Southeastern Renaissance Conference, 1957. Advances a Christian interpretation for the allegory in *Endimion*.

DORAN, MADELEINE. *Endeavors of Art: A Study of Form in Elizabethan Drama*. Madison: University of Wisconsin Press, 1963. Erudite, comprehensive treatment of the subject.

FEUILLERAT, ALBERT. *John Lyly: Contribution à l'Histoire de la Renaissance en Angleterre*. Cambridge: Cambridge University Press, 1910. Remains the best source for biographical information.

HILLIARD, STEPHEN S. "Lyly's *Midas* as an Allegory of Tyranny," *Studies in English Literature*, XII (1972), 243-258. Argues that the two plots are unified by a common concern with tyranny.

HOLZKNECHT, KARL J. *Outlines of Tudor and Stuart Plays 1497-1642*. New York: Barnes and Noble, 1947. Contains extensive plot summaries of *Campaspe* and *Endimion*.

HOTSON, LESLIE, ed. *Queen Elizabeth's Entertainment at Mitcham*. New Haven: Yale University Press, 1953. Attributes the entertainment to Lyly.

HUNTER, G. K. *John Lyly: The Humanist as Courtier.* London: Routledge and Kegan Paul, 1962. Excellent critical and historical study of Lyly's work and milieu.

HUPPÉ, BERNARD. "Allegory of Love in Lyly's Court Comedies," *English Literary History,* XIV (1947), 93-113. Attempts to interpret four of the plays as allegories of love.

KING, WALTER N. "John Lyly and Elizabethan Rhetoric," *Studies in Philology,* LII (1955), 149-161. Defends Lyly against charges that he sacrificed logic to rhetorical frills.

KNIGHT, G. WILSON. "Lyly," *Review of English Studies,* XV (1939), 146-163. Stresses sexual attraction as a theme in Lyly's works.

MINCOFF, MARCO. "Shakespeare and Lyly," *Shakespeare Survey,* XIV (1961), 15-24. Indicates that Lyly was unable to take comedy as far as Shakespeare because he was bound by artificial codes of love.

ONG, WALTER, S.J. "Tudor Writings on Rhetoric," *Studies in the Renaissance,* XV (1968), 39-69. Excellent account of the educational forces that produced Elizabethan eloquence.

PARKS, GEORGE B. "Before Euphues," *Joseph Quincy Adams: Memorial Studies,* ed. James G. McManaway, *et al.* Washington: Folger Shakespeare Library, 1948. Considers *Euphues* as a psychological novel published near the end of a tradition of prose fiction.

PARNELL, PAUL E. "Moral Allegory in Lyly's *Loves Metamorphosis,*" *Studies in Philology,* LII (1955), 1-16. Suggests that the allegory is playful and should be approached with a wayward imagination.

PARR, JOHNSTONE. "Astrology Motivates a Comedy," *Tamburlaine's Malady and Other Essays on Astrology in Elizabethan Drama.* University, Alabama: University of Alabama Press, 1953. Discusses Lyly's handling of astrology in *The Woman in the Moon.*

POWELL, JOCELYN. "John Lyly and the Language of Play," *Elizabethan Theatre,* ed. John R. Brown and Bernard Harris. London: Edward Arnold, 1966. Argues that in Lyly's works the emphasis is on figures of thought, on definition and exploration, on thinking not on feeling.

PRICE, HEREWARD T. "Shakespeare and His Young Contemporaries," *Philological Quarterly,* XLI (1962), 37-57. Unflattering presentation of Lyly's dramatic abilities.

RINGLER, WILLIAM. "The Immediate Source of Euphuism," *Publications of the Modern Language Association,* LIII (1938), 678-686. Finds the source in the academic lectures of John Rainolds of Corpus Christi College, Oxford.

162

JOHN LYLY

SACCIO, PETER. *The Court Comedies of John Lyly*. Princeton: Princeton University Press, 1969. An intensive examination of *Campaspe* and *Gallathea*.

SANDBANK, SHIMON. "Euphuistic Symmetry and the Image," *Studies in English Literature*, XI (1971), 1-13. Claims that an impulse toward rhythm, not analytical thought, occasions Lyly's Euphuistic style.

STEVENSON, DAVID L. *The Love-Game Comedy*. New York: Columbia University Press, 1946. Balanced view of Lyly's erotic comedies.

TANNENBAUM, SAMUEL A. *John Lyly: A Concise Bibliography*. New York: S. A. Tannenbaum, 1940. Useful but frequently inaccurate.

TILLOTSON, GEOFFREY. "The Prose Style of Lyly's Comedies," *Essays in Criticism and Research*. Cambridge: Cambridge University Press, 1942. Argues that Lyly fuses stylistic means with thematic purpose.

TURNER, ROBERT Y. "Some Dialogues of Love in Lyly's Comedies," *English Literary History*, XXIX (1962), 276-288. Focuses on Lyly's conversations used to dramatize love.

WILSON, F. P. *The English Drama 1485-1585*, ed G. K. Hunter. Oxford: Clarendon Press, 1969. The most recent, and the best, coverage of the drama of the hundred years before Lyly.

WILSON, J. DOVER. *John Lyly*. Cambridge: Macmillan and Bowes, 1905. Dated in many respects, but still worth examination.

Index

(The works of Lyly are listed under his name.)